ORCHIDS
of JAMAICA

ORCHIDS
of JAMAICA

A. GLOUDON
C. TOBISCH

The
PRESS
University of the West Indies

Barbados • Jamaica • Trinidad and Tobago

The Press University of the West Indies
1A Aqueduct Flats   Mona Campus
Kingston Jamaica W I

ISBN 976 640 002 4

01 00 99 98 97 96 95   6 5 4 3 2 1

Cover and book design by **Dennis Ranston**

Colour separations by **Cutting Edge Media Services Limited**

CATALOGUING IN PUBLICATION DATA

Gloudon, Ancile
Orchids of Jamaica / Ancile Gloudon,
Cicely Tobisch

p. cm.
Includes bibliographical references and index.
ISBN 976 640 002 4
1. Orchids - Jamaica - Varieties.
2. Orchids - Jamaica - Classification.
1. Tobisch, Cicely. II. Title.
QK495.064G66 1995   584. 15 dc – 20

Set in 11/13 Century Schoolbook x 26

Manufactured in Japan and Korea.

Dr C. Dennis Adams

This work is dedicated to Dr C. Dennis Adams in gracious acknowledgement for his invaluable assistance.

Photo/Illustration Credits

(by page number)

Anita Aldrich 163
Klaus Ammann 32, 55, 71, 92, 123, 200
J. Bristol 65
Ryal Chaves 47
W.F. Fant 7
W. Fawcett and A.B. Rendle (1895). Cf. *Journ. Bot.* **33: 12 -** 181
Leslie A. Garay and H.R. Sweet (1972). Cf. *Journ. Arnold Arb.* **53: 392 -** 69
Noel Gauntlett 35, 43, 54, 74, 75, 85, 135, 137, 141, 144, 155, 195, 197
Ancile Gloudon 15 *(below)*, 18, 20, 34, 38, 42, 60, 73, 77, 81, 87, 96, 98, 103, 139, 153, 157, 159, 161 *(left, right)*, 173, 179, 185, 189, 193, 204, 209
Tino Greif 40
Claude Hamilton 70
George Hart 5
K.R. and H. Jacobs 78
Ken Morgan 3, 9, 15 *(right)*, 25, 26, 37, 45, 49, 50 *(left)*, 52, 89, 99, 107, 109, 143, 170, 180, 192, 202
Alec Pridgeon 28
R. Br. (1813). Cf. Ait., *Hort. Kew. ed.* **2, 5: 211 -** 177
Schltr. (1920). Cf. Fedde, *Rep. Beih.* **7: 124 -** 105
D.L. Stevenson 11
Olof P. Swartz 147
Shaughan Terry 13, 15 *(above)*, 62, 94, 145, 149, 210
Vivian Thompson 23, 50 *(right)*, 56, 59, 64, 67, 83, 90, 101, 130, 132, 168, 176, 183, 198
Cicely Tobisch 58, 111, 112, 113, 114, 116, 117, 119, 120, 121, 122, 125, 126, 128
Dennis Valentine 22

(cover)

Ancile Gloudon (*top right, centre right*)
Noel Gauntlett (*bottom right*)
Ken Morgan (*top left*)
Vivian Thompson (*bottom left*)

Contents

DESCRIPTION OF THE SPECIES

Preface

The increasing popularity of orchid growing as a hobby world-wide has generated a marked interest in many of our Jamaican orchid species. This book has been written to heighten an awareness of the diversity and beauty of our orchid population, in the hope that with a deeper appreciation of these species, more attention will be paid to their conservation by the creation of protected orchid reserves. Happily since this manuscript was prepared, two such reserves have been established by Ancile Gloudon under the auspices of Alcan Jamaica. (See pages xviii and xix.)

The growing demand in our nation for fuel, mineral resources, lumber and living space, has put pressure on the natural forests and savannah areas where orchids grow. Consequently it is difficult to find and collect many of the rare orchid species and to protect them, in some cases, from extinction.

In this book 125 out of a possible 220 orchid species have been described in detail. All descriptions have been based on original observations made of living plants. They are accompanied by colour photographs obtained from various sources, line drawings from Garay and Dunsterville's *Orchids of Venezuela* and new line drawings produced by Cicely Tobisch.

Detailed attention has been given to the group of miniature orchids *Lepanthes* because all but one of the thirty-two species are endemic to Jamaica and are therefore important biologically and phytogeographically.

The culture notes which accompany each species description are the combined efforts of both authors based on their observations and experiences over many years. Ancile Gloudon has been growing orchids in Gordon Town at an elevation of 554 m (1800 ft) and Cicely Tobisch in Kingston at 185 m (600 ft).

The orchids in this book were selected initially from those that Ancile has found and grown over the past thirty years.

The list initially comprised 100 orchids. In the preparation of the descriptions, however, it was necessary to find the plants in bloom. In revisiting many habitats Ancile fortunately found plants that he had either neglected or had previously not identified. Unfortunately two or three plants which were on the initial list had to be omitted because, despite numerous visits to known and newly explored habitats, it was impossible to find them in flower.

Measurements have been recorded in the metric system for most of the species; plant heights, organs and floral segments are averages calculated from data compiled over a number of years from several specimens of the same species. In some cases, a range of measurements has been given when there is a relatively wide span between the lower and upper limits in the measurement of a particular character. If the plant is rare, the measurements represent those of a single specimen. If rare-blooming specimens have a multitude of flowers per inflorescence (for example, *Arpophyllum jamaicense),* it was possible to calculate averages for the floral segments. For species with minute organs and parts (for example, *Lepanthes),* the variation of a character within one or two millimetres has been considered significant and duly recorded.

This book presents a more detailed discussion of a selected number of Jamaican orchid species than appeared in "Orchidaceae" (Fawcett and Rendle 1910), and in Adams (1972). At the same time the incorporation here of cultural notes for growers provides readers with unique information not found in either of the above works.

Orchids of Jamaica is intended for the specialist as well as the orchid hobbyist, and the authors hope that their presentation will satisfy both audiences equally. Nomenclature follows that in Adams (1972) except we have deferred to Dressler (1961: 253-66) in segregating *Encyclia* from *Epidendrum.*

Acknowledgements

The consultants for this book are Professor William Louis Stern, Department of Botany, University of Florida, Gainesville, and Dr C. Dennis Adams, former Reader in Botany, University of the West Indies, Mona, author of *Flowering Plants of Jamaica* and *The Blue Mahoe and Other Bush: An Introduction to Plant Life in Jamaica,* who is currently with the British Museum (Natural History) in London.

Professor Stern has been our consultant from the outset. His attentiveness and general helpfulness (including the loan of a binocular microscope negotiated between his institution and the University of the West Indies) have been of great advantage in the production of this work.

As co-consultant Dr Adams has brought to the work a knowledge of the Jamaican orchid species, offering a reliable source of information and authoritative guidance in the identification of the species and assessment of the hybrid swarms. His loan of a large collection of photographic slides of the species was invaluable for identification purposes and for selected reproduction in the book.

The authors are grateful to Professor Richard Evans Schultes for permission to use his derivations for the names of orchid genera.

The authors appreciate the interest and help of the late Dr Lloyd Coke, Department of Botany, University of the West Indies, Mona, who arranged the extended loan of the binocular microscope without which it would have been immensely difficult to interpret the structure of the miniature orchid species, in particular, the pleurothallids.

Special thanks are due the following people who willingly offered blooming orchid specimens from their personal collections for description and photography: Elfriede Burnett, Alma Chung, Noel Gauntlett, Dr Shaughan Terry and Wolfgang Kahn. We are grateful to those who helped to type the manuscript at various stages: Caroline Burnett, Carol

Marshall and Christine Soanes of Jamaica and Sharon Cauley and the late Wendy Knowles of the University of Florida.

Ancile wishes to thank Ralph Guevara, his first botany teacher, who was responsible for awakening his interest in orchids; and again, Dr C. Dennis Adams for encouraging him to locate various Jamaican orchids on several safaris and collaborating with him over a period of several years on their identification. He also wishes to thank Dr Aubrey Jacobs, Noel Gauntlett and Ainsley Henriques for introducing him to many different orchid localities in Jamaica, and Anita Aldrich for encouraging him to start work on this volume.

Cicely wishes to thank her mother, Mrs Amy Veitch, and husband, Albrecht Hermann Tobisch, for their cooperation and extreme helpfulness in the production of this book.

We are grateful to the staff of the herbarium of the Institute of Jamaica, especially Errol Scott, Mrs Lena Green and Homer Campbell, who helped to standardize some of the drawings of *Lepanthes*. Also we must recognize with thanks the many people who have helped on safaris and in the cultivation of the orchids in our greenhouses.

Any inadvertences in transcription and observation are strictly those of the authors.

Orchid Habitats in Jamaica

We may divide the habitation sites in Jamaica into three zones:

1. Coastal to 150 m (500 ft)
2. 150 - 900 m (500 - 3000 ft)
3. Above 900 m (3000 ft)

1. The coastal areas have orchids such as *Broughtonia negrilensis, B. sanguinea, Brassavola cordata, Oncidium luridum, O. tetrapetalum, Ionopsis satyrioides, Ionopsis utricularioides* and *Vanilla claviculata* as epiphytes or sometimes growing on rocks or in leaf mould. In addition terrestrials such as *Spiranthes lanceolata* are sometimes seen.

2. This region is by far the richest with *Arpophyllum jamaicense, Brassavola cordata, Brassia caudata, Brassia maculata, Coelia triptera, Cochleanthes flabelliformis*, various species of *Epidendrum* and *Encyclia, Oncidium pulchellum, O. tetrapetalum, O. triquetrum, Ionopsis* (2) and several other epiphytes in addition to terrestrials and the saprophytic *Wullschlaegelia aphylla*.

3. This is the home for the majority of the thirty-two *Lepanthes* species that adorn the island, home also for several species of *Pleurothallis, Epidendrum* and *Dichaeas* with such rare orchids as *Neo-urbania adendrobium* and *Liparis vexillifera* growing on the forest floor, although the former is actually an epiphyte.

There are several orchids which are found in all three zones notably *Encyclia cochleata, Enc. fragrans* and *Oncidium luridum*, with the new addition *Oeceoclades maculata* seen almost everywhere, even in dry river beds.

The most populous habitats are the Cockpit Country (west central Jamaica), St Ann, which has over half of the orchids of Jamaica, and Manchester.

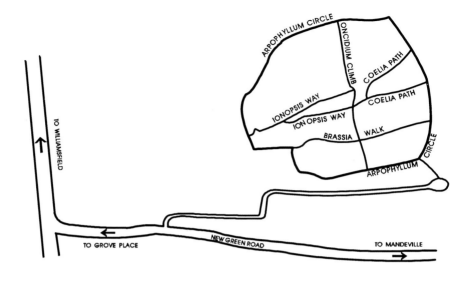

MARTIN'S HILL ORCHID SANCTUARY

Some of the hidden treasures of Jamaica are its wild orchids, many of which are unique to the island. Because of the need to conserve these species, a decision was taken to nurture and protect in centralized areas, orchids which would otherwise have been destroyed during mining. The project was born out of Alcan Jamaica Company's concern to preserve specimens of our beautiful floral heritage. Mr Ancile Gloudon, an orchidologist, proposed, developed and implemented the programme in conjunction with the company's Agricultural Division.

The collecting area for this sanctuary was western Jamaica. It occupies a little more than 0.4 hectares and has 725.3 m of well laid out trails. There are 30,000 plants in 101 species (Jamaica has 212) and 72 genera. There are 24 (out of 66) endemic orchids and 20 rare and very rare orchids, including *Epidendrum scalpelligerum* which had not been seen for over 17 years; and *Arpophyllum jamaicense* which has not been recorded as coming from western Jamaica before this exercise. There is therefore a rather good sampling of the orchid flora of Jamaica. Overall loss since the establishment of this sanctuary is calculated at less than 2 1/2 per cent – a loss rate which attests to the suitability of the site.

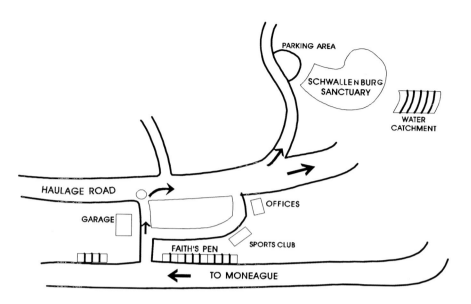

SCHWALLENBURG ORCHID SANCTUARY

About 15,000 plants in 58 species and 30 genera are located in this sanctuary. Among the species here are some of the most beautiful of Jamaican orchids such as *Broughtonia sanguinea*, *Encyclia cochleata* (the first orchid to bloom at Kew Gardens) and *Encyclia fragrans*. All these plants were collected from the Alcan mining area at Ewarton, two exceptions being species not found in sufficient quantities to allow for positive statement. There are also three "escapees": *Phaius tankervilleae*, which came from India (cf. main body of text under this name), *Dendrobium crumenatum* (pigeon orchid), which came from someone's garden (originally from India) and *Oeceoclades maculata*, which came from West Africa c. 1953, when a red dust haze covered the Caribbean basin. The Schwallenburg santuary occupies 1.6 hectares and has 2,500 m of well laid out trails. Permission to view this and the Martin's Hill sanctuary can be obtained by contacting:

Alcan Agricultural Division
3 Brumalia Road
Mandeville
Tel: (809) 962 2221

Introduction
Professor William Louis Stern

The Orchid Family

Orchids constitute a major family (*Orchidaceae*) of flowering plants and one authoritative source estimates between 20,000 and 25,000 species. They are cosmopolitan in distribution and range from north of the Arctic Circle to Tierra del Fuego in the southern hemisphere.

Orchids are most abundant as epiphytes in the tropics and subtropics but in more northerly and southerly climes they only occur rooted in the ground. The most severe deserts lack orchids as do the frigid tops of the highest mountains.

Jamaica, with its tropical climate, great range of elevations and exposures, diverse habitats, and variable spectrum of precipitation is home to more than 60 genera and 220 species of orchids. This assortment of environmental conditions allows for an orchid population which reflects a broad array of both vegetative and floral form. The largest genera in terms of native species are *Pleurothallis* and *Lepanthes*. Almost 30 per cent of the orchid species are endemic to the island, and in the genus *Lepanthes* virtually every species occurs only in Jamaica.

Most orchids are perennial herbs, although there are some which reach decidedly woody proportions. The plants assume numerous shapes and grow in different ways. Most, as noted above, are *epiphytes* and grow attached by their roots to some form of support such as tree limbs or even fence posts. Others grow over rocks (lithophytes) and still others root in the soil (terrestrials) or find a home for their roots in the leaf litter covering the forest floor.

Some orchids thrive in rather dense shade, others in the mossy dells of the high mountain cloud forests, and still others inhabit the sunlit branches of dry thorn and scrub forest shrubs and trees. Most Jamaican orchids are epiphytes, but many are lithophytes or are found sprawling about in the humus over the forest soil; a number are true terrestrials being well rooted in the earth.

Most orchids bear one or more leaves, but among Jamaican orchids there are some which are leafless or almost so. These plants must depend upon structures other than leaves for the production of food. Orchid roots are covered with a peculiar layer of tissue, the *velamen* which in the epiphytic form is white, grey or greenish and serves primarily to absorb water and dissolved minerals. In some of the leafless forms of orchids, however, most of the food manufacture *(photosynthesis)* of the plant is carried out by cells in the cortical layers beneath the velamen, and as a result these roots are rich in green colouring material *(chlorophyll)* necessary for the conversion of the sun's energy to chemical energy. In other leafless forms, for example *Vanilla claviculata,* a vining orchid, the stem is greatly elongated, thick and green, and serves as the main food-producing structure.

The stems of orchid plants are marvellously varied. Some, such as the *Vanilla* mentioned above, have clambering stems, the tough roots serving to hold the weak stems to a support, such as a tree. In some of the rooted terrestrial forms the stem is thickened and bulb-like as in *Bletia florida* and may be situated at or below ground level. In the epiphytic *Schomburgkia lyonsii* and *Encyclia cochleata,* for example, the leaf-bearing portion of the stem is inflated and stores food and water. This structure is termed a *pseudobulb* and is common in many of the epiphytic orchids. In others such as *Epidendrum verrucosum* and *Epidendrum nutans,* the leaf-bearing stem is reed-like. In the leafless *Dendrophylax funalis* the stem is greatly foreshortened and the green roots sprout from it like spokes to adhere to the supporting tree or rock.

In most epiphytic and lithophytic orchids, and in some terrestrial forms, the leaf- and flower-bearing stems arise from a more or less thickened, non-leaf-bearing stem called a *rhizome.* The rhizome also bears roots and is frequently non-green and scaly.

Orchid plants grow by one of two methods, usually designated *sympodial* and *monopodial.*

Sympodial growth takes place when the growing end of a rhizome is arrested by the production of a stem.This is usually borne at a sharp angle from the rhizome and effectively terminates its elongation. However, once the stem has flowered, one or more buds at the stem/pseudobulb base, where the shoot has branched from the rhizome, become activated and form a new rhizome which proceeds to elongate and to poduce another stem at its farther end, again terminating growth.

Monopodial growth, by contrast, requires the continued production of a leaf- and flower-bearing stem and there is no rhizome. The tip of the stem in this system of growth continues to elongate producing further leaf-bearing stems. In the monopodial method, branches bearing flowers are produced at *nodes* from the angles (*axils*) of the leaves just above where they are attached to the stem. Here there is no periodic cessation of growth and stem elongation continues uninterruptedly depending upon the peculiarities of the species in question. Roots as well as leaves usually arise from the stem at nodal regions.

Almost all Jamaican orchids grow by the sympodial method. *Vanilla, Campylocentrum* and *Dendrophylax*, however, grow by the monopodial method.

Floral parts of orchids, like all monocotyledons, are tripartite, that is, based on segments borne in threes. There are three parts (*carpels*) to the *ovary* and the *stigma* is trilobed; there are three *sepals* and three *petals* (one of which is modified to form a *lip* or *labellum*). The orchid flower is highly modified. The *style* and *staminal filaments,* characteristically separate structures in flowers in other groups of plants, are fused in orchids so that it is not possible to distinguish them. This fused structure is termed the *column* and is unique to orchid flowers. Towards the tip of the column there is an *anther* which bears pollen masses or *pollinia*, rather than separate *pollen grains,* usually the case in non-orchidaceous flowers. There may be two, four, six or eight pollinia in diffrent groups of orchids. The anther is covered by a flap of tissue, the anther cap. The *stigmatic surface* is located on the underside of the column and is separated from the pollen-bearing column tip by a flange of tissue called the *rostellum*.

Both petals and sepals in orchid flowers are usually large and coloured alike. These organs are frequently showy and ornamented in various ways. The lip or labellum is a special, highly modified petal which is ordinarily the most prominent part of the flower. In most orchids, the lip is lowermost in the flower, the so-called *resupinate* orientation. In the bud the lip is uppermost, but during the development of the flower, the flower stalk (*pedicel*) twists through 180° bringing the lip to the lowermost position in the open flower. There are however quite a number of orchid species in the Jamaican flora in which the lip is uppermost (*non-resupinate* flower), for example, *Encyclia cochleata, Encyclia fragrans* and *Polystachya concreta*. Lip, column and other floral parts may be ridged or warty, winged or eared, fused to other segments or separate.

Sometimes the column base forms a downward extension to which the lip is attached. Sepals and petals may also be affixed here. This downward extension is termed the *column foot* and in some cases the foot may be expanded into a spur-like chin or *mentum*. The presence or absence of a column foot, the placement of other parts on the column foot, and its expansion into a mentum are useful guides to orchid identification.

Orchid seeds develop from *ovules* in the ovary following pollination (which is mostly performed by insects) and fertilization. They are extremely fine, much like dust in many species, exceedingly numerous, and lack food storage tissue (*endosperm*). The successful germination of orchid seeds, and their subsequent development into leaf-bearing seedlings, depends not only on the presence of a substratum suitable for germination, but also on the simultaneous occurrence of several factors. For example, owing to the absence of endosperm to give the germinating seed a "start", the presence of a compatible fungus is essential. The fungus lives in the root tissues of the germinating seed and provides the seedling with food in the form of sugars. This is necessary for the successful growth prior to the formation of green leaves (or other food-producing organs) and the beginning of food manufacture through photosynthesis by the developing plant. In nature, this relationship (*symbiosis*) between orchid and fungus continues to endure as the plant ages and orchid roots support fungus guests throughout their lives.

Physical and Biological Features of Jamaica

The characteristics of the natural vegetation and flora of any region are dependent in large part on physical features including geographic setting, geology, topography and climate. This is particularly so of epiphytes, which sometimes rely for their existence on the presence of certain kinds of woody plant hosts (*phorophytes* or plants to which epiphytes are affixed) and of lithophytes, some of which favour certain kinds of rocks as substrata.

Also, as noted above, orchids grow symbiotically with particular fungi which play an important role in orchid nutrition. These fungi require a compatible environmental situation for their own livelihood. Thus, in order to appreciate fully the place of orchids in the landscape and to gain clues useful for cultivating them effectively, it is helpful to know something about the conditions under which they thrive in the wild.

The following pages provide information on the Jamaican environment of which orchids are a part.

Geographic Location

The island of Jamaica is centrally located in the Caribbean Sea, midway between Miami and the Panama Canal. It is part of the Greater Antilles whose other major islands are Cuba, about 144 km (90 mls) north; Hispaniola 190 km (120 mls) to the east, and Puerto Rico located east of Hispaniola, almost 800 km (500 mls) from Jamaica.

Jamaica is the third largest of the Caribbean islands. Approximately 11 250 sq km (4411 sq mls), it is 230 km (146 mls) long from east to west and 81.5 km (51 mls) wide (maximum) from north to south. Jamaica is politically divided into three counties, from east to west: Surrey, Middlesex and Cornwall. In turn each of these counties consists of several parishes:

Surrey	**Middlesex**	**Cornwall**
Kingston	St Catherine	St Elizabeth
St Andrew	St Mary	Trelawny
St Thomas	Clarendon	St James
Portland	St Ann	Hanover
	Manchester	Westmoreland

Middlesex is the largest of the counties, containing almost half the landmass of the island.

Geology

Jamaica's varied and complex landforms, wide range of soil types and differing water resources are related to its geological structure and the processes which brought this about. The distribution and configuration of its vegetation and flora are affected by the conformation and origin of the land surface.

The limestone surface which covers nearly two-thirds of Jamaica signifies its origin from the sea. The oldest known fossil-bearing rocks date to the Cretaceous period (136-65 million years ago) and were originally deposited on the sea floor as mud. This deposition was interrupted from time to time by volcanic activity, and towards the end of the Cretaceous period these rocks were invaded by granitic, igneous intrusions. Coincident with this activity, the entire area was uplifted and most, or possibly all of the island was raised above sea level. Later, much of the island gradually re-submerged and the subsequent deposits resulted in what are today the yellow limestones overlain by pure white limestones. Extensive uplifts occurred once more, accompanied by folding and faulting over much of the island.

Mountain building was especially intense towards the east where the Blue Mountains, as we know them today, were elevated to more than 2130 m (7000 ft). The limestone areas underwent considerable erosion and the softer white limestones were dissolved resulting in deeply dissected, rough terrain or karst topography which characterizes the Cockpit Country of St James and Trelawny, both parishes in west central Jamaica.

Geologically the dominant theme of central western Jamaica is limestone. Nearly 7680 sq km (3000 sq mls) are comprised of limestone, interrupted by uplifted igneous and metamorphic inliers interspersed with interior basins. The southern coastal plains are covered by alluvium overlying the limestone. Eastern Jamaica has a more complex geology of metamorphic and igneous rocks. It is here that the highest mountains occur.

Topography

The topography of Jamaica is directly related to its geologic history and the environmental forces affecting the surface of the land. Jamaica is distinguished by hills and valleys, rivers and coastal plains. Loose sandy and gravelly alluvial deposits and deltaic fans accompany the coastal plain. These alluvial deposits and deltaic fans are formed through erosion of interior rocks from the highlands and subsequent transport and deposition of eroded materials at the seashore.

There are three main types of land forms:
1. Interior mountain ranges.
2. Dissected limestone plateaux and hills.
3. Coastal plains and interior valleys.

The interior mountain ranges form the rugged spine of Jamaica and, as noted above, are highest and most craggy in the east, culminating with the Blue Mountain Peak at over 2130 m (7000 ft). In the central part of Jamaica the montains are much lower, but they are still generally deeply cleft over a large area westward from Stony Hill to the Cockpit Country.

Limestone plateaux and hills flank the higher interior ranges on all sides and occupy more than half the landmass of the island. Karst landscape, mentioned above, is especially obvious in the north central portion of Jamaica and reaches its best development in the so-called Cockpit Country.

The Cockpit Country is distinguished by numerous conical hills with precipitous sides and enclosed circular depressions (the cockpits) marked by sharp, steep slopes. The area is largely unknown botanically owing to its inaccessibility because of the treacherous terrain. Elsewhere the karst formations are more moderate and feature rolling hills, ridges, shallow sinkholes and open "knob and valley" country.

The coastal plains are most prominent on the south and narrowest on the north side of the island. The most extensive lowlands reach from the Liguanea Plains in Kingston westwards to include the plains of St Catherine and Clarendon parishes.

Other important coastal plains lie to the west in the Black River Valley of St Elizabeth and the Savanna-la-Mar area in the parish of Westmoreland. These plains are composed of alluvial deposits and as such constitute most of the rich arable soils of Jamaica. Other areas of coastal plains consist of extensive swamplands.

The Jamaican coastline is highly irregular, indented and embayed. On the north coast the bays feature white sandy beaches. The north coast is fringed with coral reefs in contrast to the south coast where reefs are few.

Climate

Jamaica lies well south of the Tropic of Cancer and the climate is characterized by warm, equable temperatures throughout the year with relatively high humidity and rainfall. However, the mountainous character of the island is responsible for a varied series of microclimates which have probably influenced the development of the diverse flora.

Northeast winds blow regularly throughout the year but are modified in their effect on the land owing to the barrier imposed by the high Blue Mountains in the east, the alternating sea breezes (onshore during the day) and land breezes (offshore during the night) and occasional cold fronts reaching their icy hands south from the American mainland during the winter.

Temperatures at lower elevations near the sea are warm with only small seasonal daily changes and average 36.7° C (90.7° F) in July with an average low of 27° C (75° F), and 34.2° C (86.7° F) in January with an average low of 23° C (69.1° F). Because of the distance of the moderating effects of the sea, there is a slightly greater range of temperature variation inland.

Temperatures are considerably cooler in the highlands: at Cinchona Hill Botanical Gardens in the Blue Mountains, for example, elevation 1490 m (4890 ft), the average high temperatures are 26.3° C (74.1° F) in July and 23.3° C (67.7° F) in January; average lows are 17.3° C (59.6° F) and 13.6° C (53.8° F), respectively. The peaks of the Blue Mountains occasionally have light frost.

Summer and fall bring the highest rainfall. The major dry period is from January to March. Although the average rainfall for the island is 196 cm (77 ins), rain does not fall evenly owing to the varied terrain. For example, the warm moisture-laden trade winds are forced upwards to the cooler reaches of the highlands where they release their watery burden. The northeast or windward side of the island receives most rainfall, an average of 254 cm (100 ins) annually. In contrast, the southern coastal lowlands are in the rain shadow area of the mountains and receive under 75 cm (30 ins) a year. The leeward plains of Pedro, along the southwest coast, and Liguanea, in Kingston, have been known to be rainless between December and July.

Vegetation

The dominant characteristic of Jamaica's landscape is its green mantle of vegetation. Before the advent of settlement by Europeans, it is probable that most of this vegetation was forest with evergreen trees in the wetter, upland areas of the northeast and deciduous scrub in the drier, lowland areas of the south and southwest. Although remnants of original mountain forests still remain, it is evident that the activities of man which have altered the environment have greatly diminished an earlier, more widespread cover of forest trees and their associated vegetation type (including epiphytes, many species of which comprise orchids). Herbaceous, coastal swamp and shore-fringing mangrove woodland, which still occur extensively, are more nearly likely to resemble the original vegetation of those areas owing to the uncultivable character of the sites.

Forests and forest reserves exist mostly in regions of mountainous terrain or areas such as karst which are largely inaccessible for habitation or uneconomical for agricultural pursuits. The northern slopes of the Blue Mountain Range, where the annual rainfall is more than 254 cm (100 ins) and there is no dry season, are characterized as Lower Montane Forest from about 609 m (2000 ft) to 1060 m (3500 ft) in elevation. The vegetation there is dense and plantation forestry is limited by the steep topography.

In parts of the southern and the drier side of the Blue Mountains between 609> m (2000> ft) and 1220> m (4000> ft) elevation is Montane Sclerophyll and open shrubby vegetation at its lower levels, which becomes an evergreen thicket higher up. This area possesses considerable attractiveness for plantation forestry. Major native trees include Santa Maria (*Calophyllum calaba*), timber sweetwood (*Nectandra coriacea*) and yellow sweetwood (*N. antillana.*).

Wet limestone forest occurs on limestone rock where annual rainfall ranges from 190 - 380 cm (75 - 150 ins), mostly at inland elevations from 305 - 860 m (1000 - 2500 ft). This is the typical Cockpit Country forest in the western and central parts in the island. Major forest trees include Santa Maria (*Calophyllum calaba)*, breadnut (*Brosimum alicastrum*), sweetwoods (*Nectandra* spp.) and bullets (*Bumelia* spp.)

The dry limestone Scrub Forest occupies rocky limestone hills, mostly under 860 m (2000 ft) elevation, where the average annual rainfall is under 100 cm (40 ins). This is the xeric thorn vegetation of low trees and tall shrubs typical of the southern coast — for example, Portland Ridge and the Hellshire Hills. Major woody species include red birch (*Bursera simaruba)*, logwood (*Haematoxylum campechianum*) and acacias (*Acacia* spp.).

Conservation of the Environment

As will be abundantly obvious to any sensitive person visiting Jamaica's forests, much of the native arborescent vegetation in the highlands has been and is being cut to make way for agriculture in the form of coffee plantations and exotic trees such as Caribbean pine *(Pinus caribaea)* and Honduras mahogany *(Swietenia macrophylla)*.

Removal of native trees and associated vegetation may alter the environment to such an extent that many native plants, especially epiphytes such as orchids, can no longer inhabit the area. The same is true of the native fauna, especially birds, which are dependent for food on native plants or on insects, and other animals which live in association with native plants.

Removal of original vegetation, especially on steep mountainous slopes, invites erosion and the subsequent, irreversible destruction of the land itself. No environmental holocaust is more devastating, nor longer lasting than that caused by removing the original plant cover which evolved over thousands of years into a finely tuned, self-perpetuating, delicately balanced ecosystem.

Map of Jamaica

ARPOPHYLLUM

From the Greek *harpe*, sickle or
scimitar and *phyllon*, leaf; alluding to
the sickle-shaped leaves of the type
species.

Arpophyllum jamaicense

Description *Arpophyllum jamaicense* is an epiphytic plant
with erect, unifoliate pseudobulbs arising from a horizontal
rhizome. The pseudobulbs are narrow, flattened, ribbed and
have three nodes with a leathery scale leaf at each node.
They are up to 40 cm tall. The leaves are linear-acuminate,
leathery, folded at the base and are up to 72 cm long and about
3 cm wide.

The inflorescence is a dense cylindrical spike up to 28 cm
long jutting out at an acute angle from the axil of the leaf,
bearing numerous flowers arranged in several rows. The
peduncle is sheathed by a tubular leathery bract.

The flowers are small, pale lavender and borne on pedicels
about 8 mm long. The petals are narrower than the sepals and
spread out horizontally; they are ovate and recurved at the tips.
The lip is amethyst, scoop-shaped, dilated at the base to form
a small pouch and has upright lateral lobes encircling the

column; its margin is slightly fimbriate. The column is tinged with amethyst at the apex.

	Length (cm)	Width (cm)
Median sepal	0.6	0.3
Lateral sepal	0.7	0.3
Petal	0.6	0.2
Lip	0.7	0.3
Column	0.3	0.1

Flowering period   March to May.

Distribution   Endemic. Stony River, Joe Hill near Corn Puss Gap, Fairy Glade, Johnson Mountain and Foxes' Gap.

Cultural notes   Basket culture is recommended using charcoal and a top dressing of sphagnum moss. Keep cool and well shaded.

BLETIA

Bletia was named in honour of Luis Blet, an eighteenth century Spanish apothecary who had a botanical garden in Algeciras.

Bletia florida

Description *Bletia florida* is a terrestrial plant with flattened, round corms, each with a diameter of about 5 cm, from the base of which hairy, whitish roots arise. Each corm has about three nodes and is covered by thick, brown sheathing scale leaves when mature. The leaves are plicate, linear-elliptic, light or dark green, may be longer than 50 cm and up to 10 cm wide. They have stiff, strong, overlapping petioles and grow from the apex of the corm but shrivel away when the plant blooms. Occasionally one or two fresh leaves may be found at this time.

The scape arises from one of the nodes of the corm and may be purple or green with purple streaks. It is jointed with small bracts at the nodes and sometimes bears a branched raceme with many dark royal-purple flowers. The lateral sepals are spreading and recurved at the tips. The median sepal is linear-lanceolate. The petals are ovate, overlap each other laterally and shield the column which protrudes forward from the centre of the flower.

The lip is four-lobed, the lateral lobes being whitish at the base with rounded margins; the front lobes have a crenulate margin and are separated by an anterior cleft. Five wavy, cream-coloured crests line the disc of the lip, the three median ones being longer than the outer two. In some clones the outer crests remain short and indistinct. The column is curved and has two lateral lobes at the apex and two auricles near the base; the inner surface is streaked with white.

	Length (cm)	Width (cm)
Median sepal	2.0 - 2.3	0.8
Lateral sepal	1.8 - 2.0	0.8
Petal	2.0 - 2.1	0.9 - 1.0
Lip	1.8	1.4 - 1.8
Column	1.5	0.4 - 0.5

Flowering period February to May.

Distribution Found mostly in eastern parishes but also in Mason River Savanna, St Ann, Manchester and Moneague in Jamaica. Also found in Cuba.

Cultural notes Any terrestrial mix may be used but the addition of limestone is beneficial. Keep in a well illuminated area.

Bletia purpurea

Description *Bletia purpurea* is a terrestrial plant with corms about 4.5 cm in diameter, covered by overlapping scale leaves with a few hairy roots sprouting from the base and bearing two to several leaves with overlapping petioles. The leaves are plicate, lanceolate-elliptic with tapered apices and stiff petioles about 10 cm long. They vary in length and are up to 1 m long (and sometimes much longer) and are between 4 and 10 cm wide.

The purple scape is jointed, may be branched and up to 1 m tall and taller. It has long internodes with short papery bracts at the nodes. The flowers vary in colour from shades of lavender to purple. An alba form is also known. The sepals are recurved at their tips and form a triangle around the petals and lip. The median sepal is lanceolate, the lateral sepals crescent-shaped and apiculate. The petals are concave, ovate-apiculate and overlap to form a hood above the column; they have amethyst nerves.

The lip is four-lobed with rounded, apiculate lateral lobes which have amethyst nerves and are separated from the paired anterior lobes by a narrow isthmus. The anterior lobes have a crenulate margin. The lip has seven to nine calli, three of them extending to the front lobes. The column is white and is extended into a foot at the base of the flower.

	Length (cm)	Width (cm)
Median sepal	2.0 - 2.4	0.6 - 0.7
Lateral sepal	1.6 - 2.3	0.8 - 0.9
Petal	1.7 - 2.1	1.0 - 1.2
Lip	1.4 - 1.9	1.2 - 1.3
Column	1.1	0.5

Distribution Sligoville, Bellevue, Newcastle, Guava Ridge, Manchester, Bull Head Mountain, Mason River Savanna, Stettin, Wait-A-Bit, Dolphin Head, Port Antonio, Negril Beach, Clydesdale, Morse's Gap and Silver Hill Gap in Jamaica. Also found in Florida, from Mexico to Panama, Venezuela, Colombia, Cuba, Hispaniola and Barbados.

Flowering period February to May.

Cultural notes The same guidelines should be used as for *B. florida* but the secret to successful growing is to expose the plants to full sunlight.

Hybridization One hybrid has been registered, that made with *Chysis bractescens* to form a *Chyletia*.

BRASSAVOLA

Brassavola honours Antonio Musa Brassavola, a sixteenth century Italian botanist and physician; professor at Ferrara.

Brassavola cordata

(Lady of the Night)

Description *Brassavola cordata* is an epiphyte with a creeping rhizome which gives rise to a dense matting of thick, fleshy, white roots which become greyish-green at maturity, sometimes tinged with pink. The rhizome branches at very short intervals, producing at each node a solitary leaf borne on a slender, terete, jointed stem up to 16 cm long, sometimes longer, which is protected by silvery membranous scale leaves. The leaves are pendulous, thick, semi-terete, with a grooved upper surface, tapering at the apices and either dark green or heavily blotched with dark purple pigments, 20 - 30 cm long and 1.3 – 1.8 cm wide.

The flowers are borne in racemes arising from the axils of each leaf in groups of four to five, or eight to fourteen or sixteen.The sepals and petals are pale green, linear-lanceolate and slightly twisted curving basally towards the centre of the flower; the petals tend to curl backwards at their tips. The lip is white or cream, sometimes with a tinge of green, cordate, with a claw about 1.7 cm long folded above the column with the upper margins closely appressed. The flowers have a heavy sweet fragrance, but only at night, hence the vernacular name "Lady of the Night".

There are apparently two varieties of *Brassavola cordata* in Jamaica. The first, found mainly in the eastern to central parishes of the island, has shorter leaves and inflorescences and ten to sixteen flowers with a leaf length of about 20 cm. The second, mainly in western Jamaica, has longer leaves up to 38 cm long and more, but with markedly fewer and larger flowers, about five to seven per inflorescence. Average leaf length is about 30 cm. Another difference is that those plants found in the west tend to have pendent leaves while those from the east have more or less erect ones.

	Length (cm)	Width (cm)
Median sepal	3.9 - 4.4	0.4
Lateral sepal	4.0 - 4.3	0.4 - 0.5
Petal	3.5 - 4.2	0.2 - 0.25
Lip	3.3 - 3.6	1.6 - 1.8
Column	0.7	–

Flowering period September to February.

Distribution Widespread throughout the island, especially on old guango (*Samanea saman*) trees. Occurrence of this species in mainland tropical America has not been confirmed.

Cultural notes Plant does well on slabs of tree fern root or woody stems of trees with exposure to strong light of at least 4000 foot candles. Plants are susceptible to mealy bug damage if neglected.

Hybridization *Brassavola cordata* has not been used in hybridization as often as other members of the genus but it has been crossed with *B. glauca*.

BRASSIA

Brassia was named by Robert Brown for William Brass, an English botanical illustrator of the eighteenth and nineteenth centuries, who collected plants for Sir Joseph Banks in West and South Africa.

Brassia caudata

(Tailed Spider Orchid)

Description *Brassia caudata* is epiphytic and frequently grows in leaf mould on the forest floor and sometimes on rock outcrops. Plants have rhizomatous stems branching from the bases of older ones, each bearing a flattened, spindle-shaped, slightly ribbed pseudobulb. The pseudobulbs are up to 10.5 cm long and average 2.75 cm wide, each bearing two or three lanceolate leaves up to 30 cm long and 3.8 cm wide. Both pseudobulbs and leaves are a glossy light or dark green. Overlapping scale leaves cover most of the pseudobulb, the uppermost pair being the longest.

The inflorescence, borne in the axil of one of the innermost scale leaves, is up to 18 cm long and bears flowers in an alternate arrangement covering most of its length. The flowers are borne on 1.3 - 1.4 cm pedicels which curve upwards from the peduncle in a phalanx formation. The petals and sepals are greenish-yellow with irregular reddish-brown spots. The sepals are dorsally keeled and lanceolate, the apices drawn out into fine filaments. The lateral sepals spread outwards on either side of the lip and hang downwards.

The petals are falcate, less than one-quarter of the length of the sepals, and together with the median sepal curve upwards in a plane perpendicular to the rest of the flower. The cream lip is ovate with a pointed apex and has a few brown blotches bordering two linear calli (5 mm long) found at the centre of the base. The natural spread of the flower is 5 - 6.3 cm with a length of 12.5 - 15 cm.

	Length (cm)	Width (cm)
Median sepal	4.2	0.5
Lateral sepal	5.1	0.5
Petal	1.8	0.4
Lip	2.4	1.1
Column	6.0	–

Flowering period May to August.

Distribution   In hilly areas above 605 m (2000 ft) in the Cockpit Country, in the parishes of Manchester, St Ann, Trelawny and St James in Jamaica. Also found in Cuba, Hispaniola, Trinidad, Mexico, South Florida and northern South America.

Cultural notes Plants on tree-fern slabs do not grow as well as plants in baskets. A fair amount of light, similar to that for cattleyas, is necessary for good growth.

Hybridization This plant has been used to make hybrids with other brassias, miltonias and oncidiums.

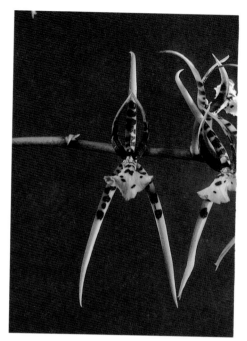

Brassia maculata

(Spotted Spider Orchid)

Description *Brassia maculata*, an epiphyte often found growing in leaf mould on rocks, is similar in form to *Brassia caudata* but the proportions are larger. The pseudobulbs and leaves are dull green, each pseudobulb bearing a single leaf from the apex and two overlapping leaves at the base. The pseudobulbs are flattened, have a fairly smooth texture and a slight curvature which becomes more pronounced with water stress. They are up to 12.5 cm long, 4.3 cm wide and are borne on short branches at wide intervals along the rhizome.

The leaves are lanceolate with tapering bases, slightly leathery and folded along the midrib. Those borne at the apex of the pseudobulbs are up to 37 cm long and between 4.4 and 6.5 cm wide; the lateral leaves have a sheathing base about 4 cm long, the lamina up to 26 cm long and 4 - 5 cm wide. The inflorescence is a raceme borne in the axil of one of the lateral leaves. The peduncle is about 50 cm long in larger specimens but there is much variation according to the size of the plant.

The number of flowers range from few to many, arranged alternately in a regular formation of two rows on either side of the peduncle, and vary from cream to yellow as they age. The sepals are linear-lanceolate, have a few brown spots along their lower halves and are grooved along the midline; the median sepal is shorter than the laterals and flanked by the petals arching upwards away from the centre of the flower. The petals are arcuate with tapering apices and are heavily barred with brown proximally.

The lip has a narrow central isthmus about 1 cm wide flaring into an outer slightly puckered lobe which has a crenulate margin and recurved apex. At the base there is a golden bifid callus 0.6 cm long and 0.4 cm wide. The lateral sepals point downwards under the lip. The column bears a yellow anther cap; the receptacle is brown. Keikis (plantlets) often appear at the apex of the old pseudobulbs.

	Length (cm)	Width (cm)
Median sepal	7.0	0.6
Lateral sepal	8.0	0.6
Petal	5.2	0.6
Lip	4.0	3.0
Column	5.0	–

Flowering period April to June.

Distribution Hollymount, Hope River Valley, Mason River, the Red Light District, Manchester and St Ann in Jamaica. Also found in Belize, Honduras, Guatemala and Cuba.

Cultural notes Plants grow well in a mixture of tree fern, charcoal, and leaf mould in wooden baskets or pots with good drainage. Keep in medium shade.

Hybridization *Brassia maculata* has been used more often than *B. caudata* to form hybrids. One of the genera used was *Leochilus* to form *Brachilus*.

BROUGHTONIA

Broughtonia was named for Arthur Broughton, an English botanist and physician who migrated to Jamaica in 1783 and produced drawings of local plants.

Broughtonia negrilensis

Some authors[1] refer to *Broughtonia negrilensis* as *Laeliopsis domingensis*. There are however some differences between that plant from Santo Domingo and *B. negrilensis*.

L. domingensis has a serrated edge on the distal third of the leaf blade while *B. negrilensis* does not. Pseudobulbs of *L. domingensis* have markedly raised circular rings which are not evident in *B. negrilensis*.

A study by Joseph Arditti[2] shows the plants listed above to have different anthocyanins in their flowers, an observation which supports our contention that they are a different species.

[1] A.D. Hawkes. 1965. *Encyclopaedia of Cultivated Orchids*. London: Faber and Faber.
[2] J. Arditti. 1969. "Floral anthocyanins in some orchids." *Amer. Orch. Soc. Bull.* 38: 407-413.

Description *Broughtonia negrilensis* is epiphytic (but often found on the forest floor in leaf mould or on rocks) with flattened greyish-green, wrinkled and clustered, ovate pseudobulbs divided into unequal internodes. Each pseudobulb bears from one to three leaves which are linear, sometimes ovate; both pseudobulbs and leaves are dull green often blotched with purple pigment. The pseudobulbs overlap each other, are partially covered by thin bracts when young, and have thick white roots arising from their bases.

The leaves are stiff greyish-green, leathery, up to 15 cm long and 3.8 cm wide. The terminal inflorescence is solitary, sometimes branched, and may be longer than 80 cm with the flowers borne towards the tip in a panicle on pedicels about 3.6 cm long. The sepals are linear-lanceolate and the petals spathulate with a finely toothed margin. Both sepals and petals are pale lavender with very fine purple veins.

The lip is the largest segment of the flower and is oval when spread out flat, but it overlaps at the base enfolding the column and forms a narrow tube which expands anteriorly. The tubular section of the lip is white and this widens into a fluted, scalloped lobe which is pale lavender, darkening into varying shades of amethyst at the border. Three to four dark purple veins mark the midline of the lip and secondary veins radiate from these to the outer lobe; short white hairs cover these central veins just to the edge of the tube. The column is broad at the apex, narrow at the base and concave on the ventral surface. It is white but flushed with purple at the base. The column foot is extended into a tubular nectary which is adnate to the ovary.

	Length (cm)	*Width (cm)*
Median sepal	3.5	0.6
Lateral sepal	3.2	0.6
Petal	3.0 - 3.5	1.0 - 1.5
Lip	3.6 - 4.0	2.8
Column	1.0	0.4

Flowering period Year-round with a peak period from November to March.

Distribution Endemic. Found on the southwestern coast from Luana to Negril and in the western Cockpit Country.

Cultural notes Plants grow well on tree-fern slabs or on shingles in well lit areas. They should be allowed to dry out between waterings.

NB Two pure alba forms have been found by members of the Jamaica Orchid Society.

Broughtonia sanguinea

This is one of the showiest orchid species in the Jamaica flora. It has gained increasing importance in hybridization with members of the *Cattleya* alliance (Laeliinae) over the past decade. However, in addition to its aesthetic appeal, it offers a challenge to the avid collector because of the wide range of forms and colour variants which exist.

Description *Broughtonia sanguinea* is mainly epiphytic but in some localities it is often found in leaf mould on the forest floor. The pseudobulbs are light green, fusiform, compressed, have three or four nodes, are bifoliate or occasionally unifoliate and overlap each other tightly; the new pseudobulbs overlying the dead ones in older plants. They are 3.6 - 10 cm long and 3 - 5 cm wide in mature specimens and are covered by overlapping scarious sheaths which are deciduous after flowering.

The leaves are leathery, oblong-lanceolate, dull or shiny green, apiculate, flared and overlapping at the bases. They are up to 24 cm long in larger specimens and are 3 - 3.1 cm wide. The inflorescence is terminal, sparsely branched, with flowers borne in clusters at the tips of the branches, each cluster consisting of twelve to fourteen flowers on average at the peak of the flowering season.

The flowers vary considerably in colour, size and shape, the larger flowers rarely exceeding 5 cm in span. The flower colour ranges from the palest pink through magenta to very dark red. Albino, peach and flavonoid forms also occur infrequently. The sepals are lanceolate and the petals are broadly ovate and apiculate. The variation in flower shape is correlated with the shape of the lip as the petals and sepals have a regular outline. The lip is roughly deltate or spathulate when it is tubular at the base, but it does not conceal the column as in *Broughtonia negrilensis*. The margin of the lip may be crenulate or entire and sometimes revolute; its surface may be puckered or smooth and possibly crystalline.

There may be a white or yellow triangle at the base of the lip in some flowers and this frequently has reddish nerves[1] radiating to the outer portions of the lip or ending midway on the disc. The column is short, with two reflexed lateral lobes; the

[1] These nerves are called transocular lines by C. Dennis Adams. The type of flower with the pure white triangle at the base of the lip has been observed by Cicely Tobisch in her own collection of broughtonias. For further information on broughtonias see C.D. Adams. 1970. *"Broughtonia* — A brief review." *The Florida Orchidist* 13: 8-11; and 1971. *"Broughtonia* again." 14: 101-105.

inner surface is concave and extends into a tubular nectary which is closely appressed to the ovary. The column is white or cream in albino and pale flowers, but is tinged with magenta in darker ones. The nectary is about 1.2 cm long.

	Length (cm)	Width (cm)
Median sepal	1.7	0.45
Lateral sepal	1.6	0.5
Petal	1.7	1.0
Lip	1.6 - 2.0	1.1 - 2.0
Column	0.2 - 0.6	0.6 - 0.7

Flowering period Year-round with a peak season from May till August.

Distribution Endemic. Lowland areas near the sea, Jackson Bay, Hunt's Pen, Portland Cottage, Port Maria, Drax Hall and further in the hills of Brown's Town, Lydford and the Cockpit Country.

Cultural notes Plants thrive in situations where there is plenty of light, excellent drainage and good air movement. For this reason they may be anchored to logs, wooden shingles, tree-fern slabs and driftwood. Local opinion has it that "the plants do not like their feet to become too wet".

Plants lying on a wire rack thrive until the time arrives for them to be mounted.

Hybridization *Broughtonia sanguinea* has been used in hybrids with cattleyas, laelias, schomburgkias, epidendrums, *Tetramicra* and *Diacrium* (*Caularthron*) among other genera. The earliest cross was *Diabroughtonia* Alice Hart made by W.W.G. Moir and named after his friend George Hart's wife. In this hybrid the colour of *Broughtonia sanguinea* does not quite come through, but with the darker cattleyas and laelias the colour is intensified. The most popular hybrids to date are the cattleytonias (*Broughtonia* x *Cattleya*).

Broughtonia sanguinea x negrilensis

Description Plants of this hybrid *B. sanguinea* x *negrilensis* are epiphytic and consist of flattened, fusiform pseudobulbs which have linear grooves and three nodes with overlapping, papery, whitish scale leaves. The pseudobulbs and leaves are usually dull green like those of *B. negrilensis* and are sometimes blotched with purple pigments. They vary from 3.5 - 5.5 cm long to 1.5 - 2.6 cm wide, bearing one to three leaves at the apex. The leaves are linear-ligulate, leathery, stiff and overlapping at the bases. The length may be up to 15 cm and the width varies between 2.2 and 3.4 cm.

The inflorescence is a raceme arising from the apex of the pseudobulb, sometimes branching sparsely. The peduncle may be as long as 60 cm and bears a cluster of about eight flowers at any one time. The flowers have a span of 4.5 - 4.8 cm and length between 4.9 - 5.5 cm. The colour varies between pale lilac and various shades of amethyst. The sepals are linear-lanceolate with fine veins; the petals are ovate-elliptic with crenulate margins and darker veins and often have splashes of amethyst. Basally the lip is white and tubular, the margins meeting above the column to varying degrees; here short amethyst veins flank the longer median ones which radiate into the outer lobe of the lip. This has a similar hue to that of the petals, is gently fluted and has a crenulate margin.

The distinguishing feature of the hybrid is that the white band on the lower half of the lip is often flattened out and the tubular base appears shorter than that in *B. negrilensis*. It is not characteristic of *B. sanguinea* to have a broad white basal band, thus the combination of this with the flatter lip of the latter, and other features along with the typical venation of *B. negrilensis* make the hybrid remarkable.

The column is white with a suffusion of lilac, sometimes having two amethyst veins on the underside. It is narrow at the base and extends into a tubular nectary spur which is adnate to the ovary. The column is broadened at the apex and the underside is concave.

	Length (cm)	Width (cm)
Median sepal	2.6	0.5
Lateral sepal	2.4	0.3
Petal	2.5	1.0 - 1.3
Lip	2.6	2.2 - 2.7
Column	0.5 - 0.8	0.3 - 0.5

Flowering period November to May.

Distribution Endemic. Between Black River and Negril in the parishes of St Elizabeth and Westmoreland.

Cultural notes The same cultural methods are required as for *B. negrilensis*. It is not unusual to find *B. sanguinea* x *negrilensis* growing among a cluster of *B. negrilensis* plants.

Hybridization Noel Gauntlett has made two hybrids using *B. negrilensis* x *B. sanguinea* (— *B. Jamaicense* as suggested by Dr Ruben Sauleda).

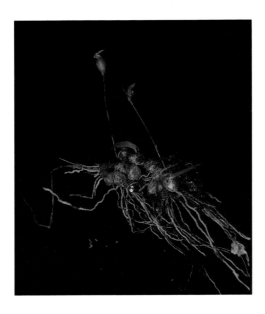

BULBOPHYLLUM

Bulbophyllum is derived from the Greek *bulbos*, a bulb and *phyllon*, a leaf; referring to the thick, fleshy leaves of most species.

Bulbophyllum jamaicense

Description   *Bulbophyllum jamaicense* is a miniature epiphytic species with a thin branched rhizome on which clustered pseudobulbs are borne and which bears fine roots radiating over the bark of the support plant. The pseudobulbs are globose, wrinkled, unifoliate and covered by scarious scale leaves; are about 0.7 cm tall and 1 cm in diameter, green with a tinge of red when young but reddish-brown after flowering has occurred.

The leaves are ovate-lanceolate, dark green, leathery, up to 2 cm long and about 0.7 cm wide. The inflorescence is a raceme bearing up to ten dark crimson flowers on a scape about 9 cm long arching some distance above the plant; it is reddish-purple, jointed with minute bracts at the nodes and zigzagged at the upper end. The sepals form a tube at the base of the flower and open slightly towards the apices. The median sepal is ovate-lanceolate, concave, with a prominent mid-nerve. The lateral sepals are arcuate and connate for two-thirds of their length.

The petals are linear-lanceolate, setose, translucent, greenish with a reddish-purple mid-vein and margin. The lip is reddish-purple, ligulate, auriculate and ciliate at the base. It is attached by a short claw to the column foot. The column is greenish and extends into a curved purplish-crimson foot; the apex is toothed and has two filamentous, branched processes.

	Length (cm)	Width (cm)
Median sepal	0.5	0.2
Lateral sepal	0.6	0.15
Petal	0.3	0.1
Lip	0.5	0.1
Column	0.1	–

Flowering period   January to August.

Distribution   Endemic. Arntully, Hollymount and the Red Light District.

Cultural notes   A rather difficult subject to handle. The plants do not thrive in cultivation but they may adapt to slab culture. If the plant is collected along with the adhering bark of the supporting tree or shrub, then this ensures minimum disturbance of the plant. Keep well shaded, cool and dry.

CAMPYLOCENTRUM

From the Greek *kampylos*, crooked and *kentron*, spur; referring to the shape of the long, slender, sharply curved spur of the lip.

Campylocentrum fasciola

(Ghost Orchid)

Description *Campylocentrum fasciola* is an epiphytic plant consisting of numerous greyish-green roots radiating up to 43 cm from a short stem, some adhering to the bark of the supporting plant. The inflorescence is branched, 3 - 8.5 cm long, and there are many inflorescences per plant. The flowers are translucent, yellowish-green and borne in two ranks on the peduncle. The sepals and petals are ovate, the petals recurved at their apices. The lip is scoop-shaped, encloses the column and is extended into a bilobed saccate green spur at the base. The column is upright and has a median projecting filament near the front.

	Length (cm)	Width (cm)
Median sepal	0.3	0.1
Lateral sepal	0.2	0.1
Petal	0.2	0.5
Lip	0.4	–
Column	0.4	0.2

Flowering period   January to March.

Distribution   River Head near Ewarton, Glen Hill, Ulster Spring, Cave Valley, Spaldings, Alexandria, Ramble (St James), Belvedere (Hanover) and Hope Bay in Jamaica. Also found in Guatemala, Belize, Columbia, Peru, Brazil, Honduras, Venezuela, the Guianas, Puerto Rico and Trinidad.

Cultural notes   The best method of cultivation is to keep the plant growing on the twig from which it was collected and place it in a shaded spot.

Campylocentrum micranthum

Description   *Campylocentrum micranthum* resembles a miniature vanda. It is epiphytic and often found anchored on twigs of trees and shrubs by long, greyish, glaucous roots which run lengthwise along the host. The shoots, freely suspended, with aerial roots sprouting from the nodes, often have stiff curved stems up to 30 cm long. The leaves are linear, stiff, leathery, dark green, deeply notched at the apices and folded at the bases, supported by ribbed sheaths which have a yellowish cast. They are 5 - 6 cm long on average and about 1.4 cm wide.

The inflorescences emerge singly through the bases of the sheaths and opposite to a leaf. They are spikes each bearing up to twenty erect flowers in two ranks. The flowers are tubular, peach-coloured at the base and cream-coloured at the apices of the perianth where they spread out to form a fringe. The sepals are narrower than the petals and apiculate. The lip is trilobed, the side lobes erect, the median lobe tapering and drawn out basally into a club-shaped spur. The column is very short. An alba form is known.

	Length (cm)	Width (cm)
Median sepal	0.4	0.1
Lateral sepal	0.4	0.15
Petal	0.4	0.1
Lip	0.35	0.2 (at base)
Column	0.25	–

Flowering period October to May.

Distribution Rather widespread on a variety of trees in Arntully, the Cockpit Country and Hollymount in Jamaica. Also found in the Greater Antilles, Trinidad, Mexico to Panama, Venezuela to Bolivia, the Guianas and Brazil.

Cultural notes The plant may be mounted on a slab or tied to a twig. Keep under light shade.

Campylocentrum pachyrrhizum
(Ghost Orchid)

Description The plant consists of fairly thick, greenish roots arising from a central leafless stem about 1.5 cm long. The inflorescence is a spike up to 5 cm long, several of which radiate from the apex of the stem. The flowers are minute and are borne in two ranks along the peduncle. The sepals and petals are ovate, cream, crystalline, and the lateral sepals overlap the petals which are basally fused with the lip to form a tan coloured saccate spur. The lip is trilobed, trough-shaped and cream with a greenish tinge at the base. The column is bright green. Each flower is subtended by a brownish bract.

	Length (cm)	Width (cm)
Median sepal	0.45	0.1
Lateral sepal	0.5	0.1
Petal	0.45	0.1
Lip	0.4	0.2
Column	0.25	—

Flowering period October to January.

Distribution Hanover, St Mary, Portland, the Cockpit Country, Moneague and the Tobolski Mines in Jamaica. Wider distribution in Guatemala, Honduras to Venezuela and the Guianas, Puerto Rico and Trinidad.

Cultural notes It is best to bind the plant to a woody twig and hang it in a cool spot.

COCHLEANTHES

From the Greek *cochlos*, snail shell
and *anthos*, flower; an allusion to the
shell-like flower.

Cochleanthes flabelliformis

Description   *Cochleanthes flabelliformis* is an epiphytic
plant sometimes found in leaf mould on the forest floor or in
rock cavities. A number of upright plantlets arise close together from a horizontal rhizome. Each plantlet has a set of
thick, soft, glabrous cream-coloured roots sprouting from the
base and bears thin, glossy, light green, ligulate leaves tapering
and folded at the bases along the midribs, overlapping each
other and spreading outwards like a fan. The leaf blades are
flattened and radiate outwards. The leaves are up to 27 cm
long and 5.5 cm wide.

The solitary flowers remain cupped when open and are borne
on peduncles up to 8.4 cm long from the axil of one of the outer
leaves. They are waxy and cream with a tinge of green. The

sepals and petals are lanceolate, pale greenish-cream and translucent.

The lip is roughly cordate with a crenulate margin and is striped with purple carinae; the lower surface is cream and the upper surface is marked with a triangle of violet-purple on the front lobe. Violet-purple carinae run from the base of the lip along the centre, radiating outwards and branching into the outer lobes to form a semi-circular ridge around the base of the lip, bordering a slight depression on the disc. The ovary is about 2.7 cm long and grooved vertically. The lip is connected by a narrow basal isthmus to the foot of the column. The column is curved slightly but with the foot perpendicular to the lip; it is greenish-cream, streaked with purple on the low surface at the base of the foot and has two small pollinia.

	Length (cm)	Width (cm)
Median sepal	3.4 - 3.5	1.2
Lateral sepal	3.1 - 3.3	1.4
Petal	3.0 - 3.2	1.1
Lip	3.2	3.4
Spur	1.4	0.7
Column	1.4	0.8

Flowering period August to March.

Distribution Banana Ground, Hollymount, Lluidas Vale, Clarendon, the Cockpit Country, St James and St Ann in Jamaica. Also found in Trinidad, the Greater Antilles and widespread throughout the mainland American tropics.

Cultural notes May be grown in baskets with crock, charcoal and tree fern in shaded conditions.

Hybridization This plant has been crossed with C. wailesiana to make C. Rosemont.

COELIA

Coelia is from the Greek *koilos*, hollow and from the erroneous idea that the pollen masses enclosed a hollow space.

Coelia triptera

Description *Coelia triptera* is lithophytic or terrestrial and occasionally epiphytic with ovate-oblong pseudobulbs, 4 cm long on average, covered basally by imbricating, papery, brown scale leaves, arising at short intervals from a rhizome, each bearing three or four linear-lanceolate leaves up to 25.4 cm long and 2 cm wide. The leaves are firm and have one or sometimes two pairs of prominent veins on the lower surface on either side of the midrib. They have tubular bases about 4 cm long which are inserted within each other at the apex of the pseudobulb.

The inflorescence is a raceme bearing numerous (eighteen to twenty-two or more) small, translucent white flowers. The peduncle arises from the base of the pseudobulb, the average height being about 10 cm, with a good portion of this length being covered by short overlapping bracts. Each flower, with its wedge-shaped ovary, is subtended by a thin membranous bract and is borne on a short pedicel, the perianth segments overlapping closely at their bases. The lip is scoop-shaped and has a depression near its base, the pointed side lobes inclining towards the column. The column is about 2 mm long and the pollinia are minute.

	Length (cm)	Width (cm)
Median sepal	0.7	0.3
Lateral sepal	0.6	0.3
Petal	0.5	0.3
Lip	0.6	0.4
Column	0.2	—

Flowering period January to March.

Distribution Arntully, the Cockpit Country, Hollymount and the Red Light District in Jamaica. Also found in Mexico, Guatemala and Cuba.

Cultural notes The best results have been obtained with an open mesh-wire basket with charcoal and leaf mould as the medium under shaded conditions.

COMPARETTIA

Named after Andrea Comparetti, an
eighteenth century Italian botanist
and professor of medicine at Padua.

Comparettia falcata

Description *Comparettia falcata* is an epiphytic plant which
is anchored to its support by very long glabrous roots which
hang freely at their tips. The plant consists of a small cluster
of linear pseudobulbs 1.5 - 2.5 cm long and about 5 mm wide,
each bearing a solitary leaf at the apex but occasionally having
another leaf sprouting from the base. The leaves are light
green, broadly elliptic, leathery, folded at the base, up to
14.5 cm long and 3.5 cm wide.

The inflorescence is pendent, sometimes branched, has a
jointed peduncle up to 45 cm long and bears up to ten flowers
arranged in two rows. The pedicels are about 1.2 cm long; the
median sepal is ovate, keeled and pink with a triangular patch
of white at the base. The lateral sepals are connate, cream-coloured, keeled and extended into a spur about 1.3 cm long at the
base.

The petals are broader than the median sepal and are pink,
blotched with white at the base. The limb of the lip is pink,

bilobed and clawed. The base of the lip has two lateral lobes flanking a white median callus and is divided into two narrow processes which are inserted into the spur, embracing the column foot. The column is white, expanded at the apex and extends into a foot at the base.

	Length (cm)	Width (cm)
Median sepal	0.9	0.4
Synsepalum	0.9	0.5
Spur	1.3	–
Petal	0.9	0.5
Lip	2.4	1.3
Column	0.6	–

Flowering period   October to March.

Distribution   Port Royal Mountains, the Cockpit Country, Hollymount, Mount Diablo, Clarendon and the Red Light District in Jamaica. A wider distribution extends from Mexico and the Caribbean through Central America to Peru.

Cultural notes   Plants flourish on tree-fern slabs which may be dressed with a little sphagnum moss to maintain some moisture and must be hung in a shaded area.

Hybridization   This plant has been crossed with oncidiums, rodriguezias and *Ionopsis*.

CRANICHIS

From the Greek *kranos*, helmet. A reference to the appearance of the flower as seen from the front, for the concave lip, borne upper-most, often projects over the callus.

Cranichis muscosa

Description *Cranichis muscosa* is a terrestrial plant which has a rosette of about four basal leaves and thick, white, hairy roots sprouting from the base. The basal leaves have grooved petioles 3 - 3.5 cm long, are ovate, apiculate, soft-textured, with bright, shiny green adaxial surfaces. The leaf blades are 2 - 2.7 cm long and 3.5 cm wide. The central scape is glabrous, brownish-green, up to 24 cm long and bears a leaf at each of the lower nodes, the internodes being covered partially by green sheathing bases of the leaves.

The flowers number about forty and are clustered in a raceme at the apex of the scape. They are white, non-resupinate with pedicellate ovaries. The lip is cucullate forming a hood over the column, is fleshy and patterned with green spots on the inner surface, and flanked by two outspreading lateral sepals which are ovate and apiculate. The median sepal is narrower than the lateral sepals, ovate, apiculate and juts downwards. The petals are lanceolate and flank a spathulate median process which emerges from the base of the column. The column is white, upright, incurving at the sides and bears two pairs of pollinia.

	Length (cm)	Width (cm)
Median sepal	0.3	0.15
Lateral sepal	0.3	0.2
Petal	0.3	0.1
Lip	0.3	0.2
Column	0.15	0.1

Flowering period November to March.

Distribution Hollymount, the Red Light District, the Tobolski Mines, Silver Hill Gap, Morse's Gap, Whitfield Hall, Moody's Gap and Vinegar Hill in Jamaica. Wider distribution from Florida to Venezuela.

Cultural notes Treat like any other terrestrial and keep well shaded.

Cranichis wageneri

Description *Cranichis wageneri* is a terrestrial plant having either one or a pair of basal leaves and a bundle of fleshy, hairy roots. The leaves are ovate to subcordate with petioles up to 3.5 cm long and blades up to 7.5 cm long and 5 cm wide. They are thin and shiny and patterned with alternating bands of light and dark green with the reticulate venation showing through. The scape is pink, tinged with green near the apex and has cream-coloured bracts. A cluster of about seven small flowers is borne at the top of the scape; they have white pedicellate ovaries tinged with green. The sepals are ovate, apiculate, and the petals are linear with long thread-like marginal hairs. The lip is scoop-shaped, apiculate and cream-coloured with transverse brown nerves on either side; the lateral lobes enfold the column.

	Length (cm)	Width (cm)
Median sepal	0.4	0.2
Lateral sepal	0.3	0.15
Petal	0.3	0.1
Lip	0.3	0.2
Column	0.25	0.1

Flowering period November to April.

Distribution Hardwar Gap, St Andrew and Portland in Jamaica. A wider distribution from Mexico to Venezuela.

Cultural notes A mixture of gravel, tree fern and fine charcoal is recommended as a medium for small plastic or clay pots.

CRYPTOPHORANTHUS

From the Greek *kryptos*, hidden, *phoros*, bearing, and *anthos* flower. Normally the flowers of this genus do not spread, the sepals being united at the base of the apex, hiding the petals, lip and other floral parts within.

Cryptophoranthus atropurpureus

(Window-Box Orchid)

Description   *Cryptophoranthus atropurpureus* is an epiphytic plant which consists of a tuft of stems, each bearing a solitary leaf which is green on the adaxial surface and purple underneath. The internodes of the stems are covered by funnel-shaped scale leaves each inserted basally into the mouth of the lower one. The leaves are leathery, ovate, elliptic, tapering to a short petiole 7 - 9 cm long and 2.6 - 3.3 cm wide.

The flowers are reddish-purple and shaped like a bird's head. They are borne singly or paired on pedicels about 5 mm long and have winged ovaries. The sepals are dull reddish-purple on the outer surface and shiny on the inner one; linear-lanceolate, heavy-textured, connate at their base and at their tips, leaving a narrow slit or window on either side between the median and lateral sepals.

The petals are much smaller than the sepals and are ovate, reddish-purple, thin-textured and three-toothed. The lip is ligulate with a pointed anterior lobe and two finely pointed lateral lobes; it articulates with the end of the column foot and stands erectly against the column. The column stands about 3.5 mm tall and has a curved foot about 2.5 mm long which has two protuberances which interlock with the lateral lobes of the lip. The capsule has six pairs of winged ridges and is about 8 mm long. An alba form which is golden-yellow has recently been found.

	Length (cm)	Width (cm)
Median sepal	0.9 - 1.3	0.6 - 0.7
Lateral sepal	0.7 - 1.8	0.6 - 0.7
Petal	0.4	0.2
Lip	0.5	0.6
Column	0.25 - 0.3	–

Flowering period July to December.

Distribution Found in Hollymount, Clarendon, Manchester, St James and Foxes' Gap in Jamaica. Also found in Cuba and Hispaniola.

Cultural notes The plant may be grown in a medium of tree fern in a pot or mounted on a slab and placed in a cool area where it is exposed to a fair amount of light.

DENDROPHYLAX

From the Greek *dendron*, tree and *phylax*, guard; an allusion to the aerial roots which clasp or guard the branches of trees.

Dendrophylax barrettiae
(Barrett's Ghost Orchid)

Description *Dendrophylax barrettiae* is one of the miniature leafless epiphytic ghost orchids, so called because the plant consists of flattened greyish-green glaucous roots containing chloroplasts beneath the epidermis and which radiate from a short, concealed and leafless stem. The roots are wavy, flattened, have green tips, are firmly appressed to their support and may well extend for over 20 cm. Several scapes (about seven) may grow simultaneously from the central stem and these are jointed and slightly zigzagged with usually one flower per scape opening at any time.

The flowers are pale green and borne on pedicels 9 - 11 mm long. The lateral sepals are elliptic, the median sepal lanceolate and the petals linear-lanceolate. The lip is scoop-shaped with the base protracted into a very thin spur. The column is a flattened green, semi-circular disc fused to the bases of the sepals and petals; the anther cap is white.

	Length (cm)	Width (cm)
Median sepal	0.6	0.2
Lateral sepal	0.5	0.15
Petal	0.45	0.1
Lip	0.4	0.3
Spur	2.0 - 2.2	–

Flowering period Year-round with a peak period from August to November.

Distribution Endemic. Worthy Park and the Cockpit Country.

Cultural notes The plant is most successfully grown when it is collected on the twig or branch on which it has been living. Failing this, one may attach the plant to a cut stem of guava, calabash, ebony or to a slab of tree fern. The plant should not be kept moist, and should be given good light.

Dendrophylax funalis

(Corded Ghost Orchid)

Description *Dendrophylax funalis* is an epiphytic plant with a short stem approximately 1 cm long which bears greyish-green roots arranged in a spiral and radiating outwards, anchoring the plant with the root tips, the plant being raised in the centre to form a hump. The presence of chloroplasts in the roots indicate that the latter perform photosynthesis. Very small scale leaves are present on the stem, otherwise leaves are totally absent.

Plants often form colonies with stolons interconnecting adjacent plants. The older basal portion of stem with its complement of roots may shrivel away regenerating new growth at the apex.

The flowers are usually borne singly but sometimes in clusters of two or three on scapes 2.5 - 4.5 cm long. The ovary is pedicellate and about 2.1 cm long. The sepals and petals are pale green or cream-coloured and are attached to the base of the column at the apex of the ovary. The median sepal and petals are ovate-apiculate; the lateral sepals arcuate.

The base of the lip is a slightly flattened cone extended into a spur 3.4 - 5.1 cm long with the column attached above the aperture. The column is flattened, helmet-shaped, with two apiculate lobes curving downward inside the basal lobes of the lip and concealing the stigmatic surface. The lip is cream-coloured and has a short claw which flares out into two rounded outer lateral lobes which are separated by a deep cleft. A median crest runs along the midline of the spur on to the claw of the lip.

	Length (cm)	Width (cm)
Median sepal	2.0	0.6
Lateral sepal	2.3	0.5
Petal	1.9	0.7
Lip	2.0	2.4

Flowering period September to April.

Distribution Endemic. Arntully, the Cockpit Country, Hollymount, Worthy Park and St Thomas.

Cultural notes The plant flourishes with a good deal of light and grows well on tree-fern slabs or in a basket with charcoal and leaf mould.

DICHAEA

From the Greek *diche*, twofold and *nema*, thread; from the two processes on the column.

Dichaea glauca

Description *Dichaea glauca* is an epiphytic plant which has tufted glaucous shoots up to 37 cm long, each having the appearance of a quill. The leaves are oblong, thin, finely apiculate and glaucous on the abaxial surfaces. They are up to 6 cm long and 1.3 cm wide, and have imbricate bases which are folded so that all the laminae lie in two rows in the same vertical plane along the length of the shoot.

The flowers are crisp, cupped and crystalline white with a few reddish spots at the base of the petals and lateral sepals. They are produced singly from the axils of the leaves, protruding from the underside of the middle portion of the shoots and borne on glaucous pedicels up to 2.8 cm long.

The sepals are ovate-lanceolate and point forwards; the lateral sepals have a group of reddish spots at the base and are recurved at their tips. The petals are narrower than the sepals, linear-lanceolate and curve inwards. The lip is diamond-shaped with pointed lateral lobes; at the narrow base there is one prominent red spot flanked by two smaller ones. The column is globular.

	Length (cm)	Width (cm)
Median sepal	1.1	0.4
Lateral sepal	1.0	0.4
Petal	0.9	0.35
Lip	1.0	1.2
Column	0.5	0.3

Flowering period   June to July.

Distribution   Clydesdale, Hollymount and Johnson Mountain in Jamaica. Also found in Mexico, Guatemala, Honduras, Cuba, Costa Rica and Hispaniola.

Cultural notes   This species may be grown in a pot or wire basket in a medium of charcoal and bagasse or peat moss. The charcoal should be broken into small pieces so that the medium will retain moisture over a long period. A top dressing of sphagnum moss may be added. Keep well shaded.

Dichaea graminoides

Description *Dichaea graminoides* is epiphytic, pendent, with freely branching shoots up to 30 cm long. It has linear-lanceolate, apiculate, pale green leaves which are 2.5 - 4 cm long and about 6 mm wide arranged pinnately along the stem. The internodes of the stem are covered by the overlapping bases of the leaves; the lower nodes are anchored to the host or substratum by slender roots.

The flowers are minute, white and have a span of about 1 cm; they arise singly from the axis of the leaves on filiform pedicels about 1.9 mm long. The sepals are lanceolate and the petals ovate-lanceolate. The lip is spathulate and the column globular.

	Length (cm)	Width (cm)
Median sepal	0.6	0.2
Lateral sepal	0.6	0.25
Petal	0.5	0.2
Lip	0.35	0.35
Column	0.2	0.25

Flowering period   May to December.

Distribution   St Andrew, Portland and St Thomas in Jamaica. A wider distribution ranges from Mexico to tropical South America, Cuba, Hispaniola and Tobago.

Cultural notes   Plants should be placed in open baskets on a medium of fine charcoal and leaf mould and/or shredded tree fern. A top dressing of dried, shredded sphagnum moss may be added. Keep well shaded.

Dichaea muricata

Description   *Dichaea muricata* is epiphytic with trailing stems up to 50 cm long, sheathed by the overlapping bases of the leaves. Fine roots sprout from the base of the plant. The leaves are ovate, finely apiculate, pale green and have a soft papery texture; they are about 2 cm long and 7 mm wide and are arranged close together along the stem with all the laminae spread flat and lying in the same plane.

The flowers are borne singly on thin pedicels about 1.3 cm long and protrude from the leaf axils along the backs of the newer growth. The sepals and petals are concave, rough on the dorsal surfaces and pale tan with purple spots on the petals;

the sepals are ovate and the petals lanceolate. The lip is ovate with the margin entire, scoop-shaped with a narrow basal claw and white with purple barring. The column is flattened into a ridge at the top and the stigmatic surface has a ligule protruding upwards at the centre.

	Length (cm)	Width (cm)
Median sepal	0.5	0.4
Lateral sepal	0.6	0.3
Petal	0.6	0.25
Lip	0.6	0.4
Column	0.2	0.4

Flowering period August to January.

Distribution Fairy Glade, Arntully and Johnson Mountain in Jamaica. Also found in Trinidad, Brazil, Ecuador, Colombia, Venezuela and from Mexico to Panama.

Cultural notes The same cultural methods should be employed as for *Dichaea glauca*.

ELLEANTHUS

From the Greek *ella*, heroine of the Hellespont and *anthos*, flower; genus dedicated to Helle or Helena in whose honour the Hellespont was named.

Elleanthus cephalotes (capitatus)

Description *Elleanthus cephalotes (capitatus)* is an epiphytic plant which grows with a tuft of leafy shoots from a thick matting of glabrous roots anchoring it to its support plant. The stems are slender and reach a height of 60 cm at maturity. The leaves are plicate, linear-ovate and acuminate, 11 - 27 cm long and 3 - 5 cm wide. The blades are glossy green adaxially, puckered and convex towards the base and eventually deciduous, leaving tubular sheaths covering the lower internodes.

The inflorescence is a terminal capitulum covered at the base with tightly overlapping green bracts, the peduncle being an extension of the stem. The pedicels are about 1.2 cm long, each subtended by a stiff green bract 2.0 - 2.5 cm long and 8 mm wide basally.

The capitulum is covered at the base by tightly overlapping green bracts. The florets are tubular, amethyst and have an orbicular chin at the base. The sepals are connate basally forming a tube, but have pointed apices.

The petals are linear and appressed to the sides of the lip which completely encircles the column but flares outward from the base; the outer lobe has a crenulate margin. Basally the lip has two white glands which project into the base of the column, which is white with an amethyst suffusion and curves forward slightly. The column has a narrow "stalk-like" foot which protrudes into the small chin formed by the lip. There is some mucilage inside the perianth.

	Length (cm)	Width (cm)
Median sepal	0.9	0.3
Lateral sepal	1.0	0.3
Petal	1.0	0.2
Lip	1.4	0.1
Column	0.9	—

Flowering period   April to October.

Distribution   The Cockpit Country, Hardwar Gap, Hollymount and the St Andrew Hills above 900 m (3000 ft) in Jamaica. Wider distribution from Mexico to Panama and in Colombia, Peru and Brazil.

Cultural notes   The plant grows readily in wire baskets or pots but is not easily brought into flower. A top dressing of sphagnum moss will help to keep the plant cool. Keep well shaded.

Elleanthus longibracteatus

(Golden Shower)

Description   *Elleanthus longibracteatus* is epiphytic or li-thophytic with leafy shoots growing together in tufts, the stems slender and growing up to 100 cm tall. The leaves are lanceo-late, acuminate and up to 16 cm long and 2 cm wide; they are stiff and strongly veined with the upper surfaces a dark shiny green and the bases completely sheathing the internodes.

The inflorescence is a terminal spike 5.5 cm long with about twenty flowers arranged spirally, each subtended and partially enfolded by an acuminate bract. At maturity the flowers open slightly, the lip being uppermost. The flowers are membranous and cream becoming yellow as they age.

The median sepal lies parallel to the subtending bract, is ovate, concave and completely overlaps the column. The lateral sepals are saccate at the base and pointed at their apices. The petals are elliptic. The lip is triangular with a fimbriated anterior margin. There is a small trough-shaped sac at the base of the lip at the junction with the column and two pear-shaped glands are also found at the base. The column is curved downwards and ventrally concave.

	Length (cm)	Width (cm)
Median sepal	0.5	0.3
Lateral sepal	0.5	0.3
Petal	0.5	0.2
Lip	0.7	0.6
Column	0.4	0.4 at widest

Flowering Period   March to July.

Distribution   The Cockpit Country, Darliston, Greenwich, Hollymount and Peckham Woods in Jamaica. Also found in the Greater Antilles, Central America, Colombia, Ecuador, Peru and Bolivia.

Cultural notes   Same as for *E. cephalotes*, but with this species sphagnum moss is not necessary as the plant is more heat-tolerant and blooms readily.

ENCYCLIA

From the Greek *enkyklein*, to encircle; from the shape of the lip which encloses the column.

Encyclia angustifolia

Description *Encyclia angustifolia* is an epiphytic plant with pear-shaped, unifoliate pseudobulbs, up to 1.8 cm tall. The leaves are linear, stiff, leathery, up to 18.5 cm long and 5 mm wide. The inflorescence is a sparsely branched panicle up to 23 cm long, bearing a few flowers. The flowers are tawny yellow and are borne on pedicels about 1.2 cm long.

The sepals and petals are linear-lanceolate and patterned with linear-brown nerves, inclining towards the lip which has three linear, lavender calli flanked by two nerves, the median callus being raised. The lip is trilobate with an ovate-apiculate anterior lobe which curves downwards and ovate lateral lobes with upper margins overlapping and shielding the column, the apices curling backwards.

There is a short, glandular bilobed ridge at the base of the lip which is closely appressed to the lateral lobes of the column. The column is short and green with two brown pollinia.

	Length (cm)	Width (cm)
Median sepal	1.1	0.25
Lateral sepal	1.0	0.25
Petal	1.1	0.15
Lip	1.0	0.7
Column	0.2	0.1

Flowering period   August to September.

Distribution   The Cockpit Country, Hollymount, Christiana and Bellevue in Jamaica. A wider distribution occurs in Cuba, Mexico, Guatemala.

Cultural notes   A good subject for either pot or slab culture although the latter is better.

Encyclia cochleata

(Cockleshell Orchid)

Description   *Encyclia cochleata*, an epiphytic plant, has spindle-shaped bifoliate pseudobulbs which are somewhat flattened, slightly crinkled, up to 15 cm long, and each borne on a short stalk arising from the rhizome. Thick white roots sprout from the bases of the pseudobulbs anchoring the plant firmly to its support. The leaves are erect, linear-lanceolate, up to 30 cm long or longer and 3.4 - 3.8 cm wide.

The inflorescence is a raceme bearing six to ten flowers emerging from the apex of the pseudobulb in the axil of the upper leaf. Each peduncle is subtended by a papery brown bract at the base and has several bract-bearing nodes, the flowers being borne with the lip uppermost on arching green pedicels up to 3.8 cm long. The sepals and petals are arcuate, tapered, curling at the apices, and all project downward towards the front of the flower; they are greenish-cream and spotted with purple basally. The lip is cordate, fused along the narrow basal isthmus to the lower end of the column, the lateral lobes curving around the middle of the column to form a cockle.

The column is upright and is superimposed on two linear white crests of the lip. Basally the lip has a cream-coloured, crescent-shaped band which is striped by radiating dark purple veins extending into a bordering dark purple band. The dorsal and ventral surfaces of the lip are also dark purple. Very short, distinct purple veins project just above the tip of the column. The upper central portion of the lip has a diamond-shaped area of pale greenish-yellow stripes. There is a variability in the colouration and patterning of the labellum in specimens from other countries. A pure yellow form has been found in Jamaica. The size of the flower varies considerably according to habitat, those from shaded, moist areas being larger than those from drier areas.

	Length (cm)	Width (cm)
Median sepal	4.6 - 5.1	0.5
Lateral sepal	4.5	0.5
Petal	4.0	0.4
Lip	1.8	1.4
Column	0.6 - 0.7	0.35

Flowering period   Year-round.

Distribution   Probably the most widespread of all Jamaican orchids, this species flourishes in large colonies on old trees. Also found on bank sides and old stone walls in Manchester, St Ann, St Mary, Trelawny and St Andrew. This species also occurs in Colombia, Venezuela, Florida, other Caribbean islands and Central America.

Cultural notes   *Encyclia cochleata* grows well in baskets or on slabs, or on the stout stems of calabash (*Crescentia cujete*) or ebony (*Diospyros tetrasperma*). Keep well illuminated.

Hybridization   *Encyclia cochleata* has been crossed with epidendrums and cattleyas.

Encyclia fragrans

(Fragrant Cockleshell Orchid)

Description   *Encyclia fragrans* is epiphytic and bears fusiform pseudobulbs 6 - 10 cm long, arising alternately from a rhizomatous stem which has strong white roots. The pseudobulbs are flattened and grooved longitudinally, each one bearing a leathery, ligulate leaf which may be 22 - 35 cm long or longer and 3.5 - 4.2 cm wide. Both pseudobulbs and leaves are light, dull green.

The inflorescence is a raceme borne at the apex of the pseudobulb. The pedicels are short and fairly stout, with the flowers held uppermost, and spirally arranged around the upper ends of the peduncle. The flowers are cream-coloured with a slight tinge of green. The lip is cockle-shaped, lightly striped with purple veins, and has a narrow isthmus 4 mm long united with the back of the column. The sepals are linear-lanceolate; the lateral sepals point diagonally on either side of the lip and the median sepal points downwards.

The petals are ovate-elliptic and point outwards horizontally. The column is fused at the base to the isthmus of the lip and is closely appressed to the latter at its free upper end where it covers two linear crests. The anther bears two yellow pollinia. Several pseudobulbs on the same plant may flower simultaneously to give a mass of aromatic blossoms.

An alba form without any red lines in the lip is known.

	Length (cm)	Width (cm)
Median sepal	3.0 - 3.3	0.6
Lateral sepal	3.0	0.5
Petal	2.3 - 2.7	0.9
Lip	1.6 - 2	1.6 - 1.8
Column	0.6	0.25

Flowering period Year-round.

Distribution Widespread except in extremely hot seaside areas in Jamaica. Also distributed from Mexico and other Caribbean islands to Ecuador, Peru and Brazil.

Cultural notes Slab or basket culture may be used. Basket culture is to be recommended as it helps to curtail the somewhat spreading habit of the plant.

Hybridization Seldom used, but mainly with cattleyas to form epicattleyas, for example, *Epicattleya skigrans*.

Encyclia ottonis

Description   *Encyclia ottonis* is epiphytic with flattened, pale green, unifoliate, spindle-shaped pseudobulbs up to 2.8 cm long and 1.3 cm wide, borne on short, jointed stems arising from a branched horizontal rhizome. The leaves are linear-lanceolate, stiff, pale green, up to 14 cm long and 1 cm wide. The inflorescence, which arises from the axil of the leaf, is about 11 cm long and bears a few cream-coloured flowers.

The sepals are elliptic, apiculate and the petals are elliptic-lanceolate, forming a shield for the column. The lip is ligulate, apiculate, has a median nerve, slightly undulate margins and curves downwards. It is keeled at the apex and has a short beak. The column arches forwards in the flower. The ovary is pedicellate.

	Length (cm)	Width (cm)
Median sepal	0.9	0.3
Lateral sepal	0.9	0.3
Petal	0.7	0.25
Lip	0.6	0.2
Column	0.35	0.2

Flowering period   September to January.

Distribution The Cockpit Country, Hollymount and Ramble (St James) in Jamaica. Also found in Trinidad, the Greater Antilles and from Panama to Venezuela.

Cultural notes The plant grows best on tree-fern slabs because of its creeping habit. It should be kept in light shade.

Encyclia polybulbon

(Dinema polybulbon)

Description *Encyclia polybulbon* is epiphytic or lithophytic with a long branching rhizome bearing pseudobulbs at regular intervals and sprouting fine white roots. The pseudobulbs are spindle-shaped, 1.8 - 2 cm long, bearing two or three leaves. The leaves are ovate-elliptic, leathery, rigid, notched at the apices, up to 3.6 cm long and 1.2 cm wide.

The flowers are borne singly on peduncles which are 1.8 cm tall arising from the axils of the leaves. The flower is star-shaped with a cream, heart-shaped lip which is clawed at the base and has a prominent median vein. The sepals and petals are linear and pale cinnamon-coloured. The column is slightly longer than the claw, is striped cream and purple and has two minute processes projecting on either side.

	Length (cm)	Width (cm)
Median sepal	1.6	0.2
Lateral sepal	1.4	0.3
Petal	1.3	0.1
Lip	1.2	0.9
Column	0.7	–

Flowering period   September to March.

Distribution   Arntully, Bellevue, the Cockpit Country, John Crow Mountains, Hardwar Gap, the Red Light District, Warsop, Crofts Mountain, Peckham Woods and Christiana in Jamaica.   Also found in Cuba, Mexico, Guatemala and Honduras.

Cultural notes   Slab culture is recommended but this plant may also be grown in fine charcoal and leaf mould or bagasse under lightly shaded conditions.

Encyclia pygmaea

Description   *Encyclia pygmaea* is an epiphytic plant often found on the forest floor or on rock surfaces. It is characterized by a long branching dark green rhizome which bears single pseudobulbs at regular 3 cm intervals and is covered by brown, papery scale leaves.

The pseudobulbs are dark green, fusiform, up to 2.5 cm tall, each bearing a pair of thick ovate leaves 4 - 5 cm long and 1.5 cm wide. Each pseudobulb is covered at its base by a pair of papery brown overlapping scale leaves. One or two flowers are borne at the apex of the pseudobulb in the axil of the leaves.

The peduncle is short and the pedicels are on average 0.5 cm long. The petals are narrow, thread-like, about 0.4 cm long and pale greenish yellow. The sepals are pale green, broad at the base with very acute apices. The column is about 3 mm long and is fused to the base of the lip. The lip is white, the limb being 4 mm wide with two lateral lobes which envelop the column; the apex is sharply pointed.

	Length (cm)	Width (cm)
Median sepal	0.5	0.2
Lateral sepal	0.6	0.2
Petal	0.4	–
Lip	0.4	0.06 at widest
Column	0.2	–

Flowering period   October to April.

Distribution   The Cockpit Country, Hollymount, Lydford and the Red Light District in Jamaica. Also found in Florida, Mexico to Brazil, the Greater Antilles and Trinidad.

Cultural notes   The same as for *Encyclia polybulbon*.

Encyclia spondiada

Description   *Encyclia spondiada* is an epiphytic plant which has light green, narrow pseudobulbs with shallow grooves, between 7 - 7.5 cm long, each covered by overlapping scale leaves about 1.5cm long and borne on a branching rhizome. The leaves are linear-ligulate, have a prominent midrib, and are up to 21.5 cm long and 2.2 - 3.3 cm wide.

The terminal inflorescence is up to 9 cm long and bears only a few flowers. The sepals and petals are creamy-yellow and tipped with orange. The sepals are linear-lanceolate and the petals are elliptic, clawed at the base, and finely drawn out at the apices. The lip is sagittate, cinnamon-coloured with brown veins and bears two small basal glands. The ovary is three-winged and about 2.4 cm long.

	Length (cm)	Width (cm)
Median sepal	1.8 - 3.2	0.5 - 0.6
Lateral sepal	1.7 - 3.1	0.5 - 0.65
Petal	1.5 - 2.8	0.6 - 0.9
Lip	1.2 - 2.0	0.8 - 1.3
Column	0.5 - 0.8	0.35

Flowering period October to February.

Distribution Rare. Clydesdale, John Crow Peak, Wag Water and Ginger Rivers, Morse's Gap and the Cockpit Country in Jamaica. Also found in Costa Rica.

Cultural notes The plant may be grown on a tree fern or cork slab, or it may be potted in a medium of tree fern and charcoal. Keep in shade.

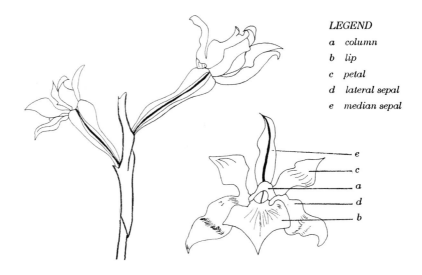

LEGEND

a column
b lip
c petal
d lateral sepal
e median sepal

EPIDENDRUM

From the Greek *epi*, upon and *dendron*, tree; upon trees, or tree-perching; from the epiphytic habit of most species in the genus.

Epidendrum anceps

Description *Epidendrum anceps* is a rather attractive plant that has a tuft of leafy shoots. The axis of the inflorescence extends up to 90 cm and longer above the leaf-bearing portion of the stem and when immature, it is completely covered with green bracts tinged with brown. This is a characteristic which is shared with some of the "reed-stem" epidendrums, for example, *Epidendrum radicans*.

The peduncles bearing one or more umbels of tiny greenish or tan-coloured flowers arise near the apex of the elongated peduncle and in some cases keikis may also be found. The leaves are up to 32 cm long and 5 cm wide, obovate, fleshy, tinged with purple and having sheathing leaf bases which completely enclose the stems, the apices pointing upwards. The leaf blades are folded basally, overlapping each other alternately with the adaxial surfaces all lying in one plane on the older stems.

The flowers are thick and waxy. The lip has a narrow basal isthmus about 4 mm long which is fused to the column and expands into a trilobed limb, there being two lateral lobes and the mid-lobe having two small points separated by a minute ridge. The sepals are ovate and the petals linear.

	Length (cm)	Width (cm)
Median sepal	0.6	0.4
Lateral sepal	0.7	0.4
Petal	0.6	0.1
Lip	0.9	0.9
Column	0.4	–

Flowering period Year-round.

Distribution Arntully, the St Thomas hills, Hollymount, Hardwar Gap, Manchester and the Cockpit Country in Jamaica. Also found in Florida and from the West Indies and Mexico to Colombia.

Cultural notes Basket or tree fern slab culture gives good results. Keep lightly shaded.

Hybridization *Epidendrum anceps* has been little used in hybridization but has been crossed with *Broughtonia sanguinea* and *E. moyobambae* (*E. coronatum*).

Epidendrum bifarium

Description *Epidendrum bifarium* is an epiphytic plant with upright stems branching sympodially and giving rise to stout glabrous roots at the base of each branch. The stems are up to 8 cm tall, stout, rigid and almost cylindrical, the internodes being covered by the tubular sheathing bases of the leaves.

The leaves are linear-ovate, apiculate, leathery, thick, stiff and bright green but sometimes bear reddish midribs, their bases encircling the stem. They are up to 7 cm long and 1 cm wide and are arranged alternately in two rows along the stem.

The inflorescence is a pendulous, flattened spike, up to 18 cm long, covered by apiculate tubular bracts and bearing up to about twelve waxy green flowers. The flowers are green and stiff and widely spaced in two rows. The sepals are ovate, apiculate, their apices pointing to the corners of a triangle, the abaxial surfaces having a suffusion of red.

The petals which flank the lip are green thread-like filaments, notched at the apices. The lip is fused to the column at its base to form a long, narrow tube, the limb having three main lobes, the median lobe being convex in the centre and subdivided into small lateral lobes. The column is fused to the lip for the entire length except at the apex where it is purple and dilated to form an aperture. The lip has two prominent green calli at the entrance of the aperture flanked by two small protuberances.

	Length (cm)	Width (cm)
Median sepal	0.5	0.2
Lateral sepal	0.7	0.25
Petal	0.3	—
Lip	0.65	0.5
Column	0.4	0.2

Flowering period   November to March.

Distribution   Found in Whitfield Hall, Vinegar Hill, Clydesdale, Silver Hill Gap, Bellevue, St Catherine's Peak, Cedar Hurst and Wallenford in Jamaica. Also found in Colombia and Venezuela.

Cultural notes   Plant in a pot or wooden basket using medium or fine charcoal 6 - 19 mm (1/4 - 3/4 ins) in size with a top dressing of sphagnum moss. Keep well shaded and cool.

Epidendrum difforme

Description *Epidendrum difforme* is an epiphytic plant which has a cluster of stout stems which are sometimes zigzagged, sometimes pendulous, and bear stiff, succulent, light green leaves which have tubular sheathing bases about 3 cm long. The leaves are oblong-ovate, keeled at the bases, notched at the apices and up to 9.5 cm long and 2.7 cm wide.

The inflorescence is a terminal umbel with a very short peduncle, the flowers of which are borne in clusters of ten to fourteen at maximum development on pedicels which are about 4 cm long. The flowers are pale green, translucent, with petals and sepals recurved. The median sepal is linear-lanceolate; the lateral sepals are arcuate and the petals linear-elliptic.

The lip has a basal isthmus about 1 cm long. This forms a tube with the column to which it is fused, and expands into a convex limb which has two lateral auricles and two short frontal lobes, the margin being crenulate. The column has a cream-coloured fringe overhanging the anther.

	Length (cm)	Width (cm)
Median sepal	1.8	0.5
Lateral sepal	2.0	0.6
Petal	1.6	0.25
Lip	2.1	2.1
Column	1.0	–

Flowering period Year-round.

Distribution Widespread on trees in savanna areas, especially on citrus and calabash. Found in Point Hill, the Mocho Mountains, Christiana, Troy, Lydford and Mosely Hall Cave in Jamaica. Also found in the Lesser and Greater Antilles, Brazil, Costa Rica, the Guianas and Venezuela.

Cultural notes Plant may be grown in a pot of shredded tree fern or it may be mounted on a slab. It takes some time for the plant to acclimatize to a new environment. Keep under lightly shaded conditions.

Hybridization This plant has been hybridized with epidendrums and diacriums.

NB There are apparently three forms of this species. One attains a height of not more than 7.5 cm and is found at elevations above 1200 m (4000 ft). This form bears three or four flowers in an inflorescence. The second is spindly, about 25 cm tall, carries about nine flowers and appears at elevations about 600 m (2000 ft). The third is rather thick-stemmed, more robust than the others, occurs at the same elevation as the second and carries up to fourteen flowers per inflorescence. The height is in excess of 50 cm in some specimens.

Epidendrum diffusum

Description   *Epidendrum diffusum* is an epiphytic plant with mature specimens differing considerably in size. The plant has zigzagged stems up to 15 cm long with swollen bases and the internodes are entirely covered by the sheathing bases of the leaves. The leaves are oblong-ovate, leathery, up to 5.8 cm long and 3 cm wide and have a reddish-purple pigment concentrated in the margins and in the veins of the sheathing bases.

The terminal inflorescence is a panicle which may be as long as 30 cm with a slender peduncle. The flowers may be few or numerous and are fragile. The sepals and lip are pale green tinged with brown. The lip has a deltate limb and a narrow claw about 3 mm long fused to the column and lies in the same plane as the underlying lateral sepals. There are apparently two colour forms, one green, the other light tan, conforming to the colour of the leaves.

	Length (cm)	Width (cm)
Median sepal	0.5	0.1
Lateral sepal	0.5	0.1
Petal	0.6	0.2
Lip	0.65	0.4
Column	0.25	—

Flowering period   July to December.

Distribution   Rather common. Arntully, the Cockpit Country and Hollymount in Jamaica. Distribution ranges from Mexico to Brazil and Cuba.

Cultural notes   Best results are obtained with slab culture under light shade.

Epidendrum jamaicense

Description   *Epidendrum jamaicense* is epiphytic with rigid trailing stems about 55 cm long which branch dichotomously at regular intervals, the older segments remaining leafless with only the topmost branches bearing leaves. The internodes are covered by papery, whitish, often discoloured tubular sheaths. The roots are sparse, glabrous and may be up to 1 m long in some instances. The leaves are bright green, thin, elliptic-lanceolate, the older ones being 7 - 10 cm long and 1.6 - 2.3 cm wide.

The inflorescence is a terminal raceme with one to five green flowers. The sepals are membranous with fine green veins; the median sepal is linear-lanceolate and the lateral sepals roughly elliptic. The petals are filamentous. The lip is fused to the lateral lobes of the column along its basal isthmus to form a tube leaving a narrow slit at the front; it has an expanded outer limb with decurved margins. The column has a pale green anther cap.

	Length (cm)	Width (cm)
Median sepal	1.6	0.5
Lateral sepal	1.5	0.45
Petal	1.4	0.15
Lip	1.7	1.3
Column	1.0	–

Flowering period May to September.

Distribution The Cockpit Country and Hollymount in Jamaica. Also found in Hispaniola and Dominica.

Cultural notes This is one of the most difficult plants to establish. They wither very soon after collection. Younger plants seem to fare better than older ones. Care must be taken to remove as much of the rooting system as possible. Plants should be attached to tree-fern slabs or placed in rather deep pots. Some sphagnum moss used as top dressing helps to keep the plants cool. Plants should be placed in a shaded spot.

Epidendrum nocturnum

Description *Epidendrum nocturnum* is epiphytic and grows up to 100 cm tall. It is often found on rocks and in leaf mould at higher altitudes 600 m (2000 ft). The stems are jointed and bear leaves only at the upper portions in older stems. The leaves are up to 11 cm long and 2 cm wide. They are obtuse and leathery and the sheathing bases which remain after the leaves have fallen become very hardened and discoloured.

The inflorescences are terminal and the flowers are borne in quick succession. The star-shaped flowers have slender sepals and petals. The sepals are pale green or olive, linear-lanceolate with the margins rolled under; the petals are linear and point downwards. There is a bifid lip which has a slender median filament 2.6 - 3.5 cm long emerging from the base of the column and separating its lateral lobes. At the base of the filament there are two raised linear calli 5 mm long. The column is fused to the base of the lip for approximately half of its length and projects for about 0.5 cm above the limb of the lip. Old peduncles continue flowering for some time. The flowers are fragrant at night.

	Length (cm)	Width (cm)
Median sepal	4.5 - 6	0.7
Lateral sepal	4.5 - 6	0.6
Petal	4.0 - 3.6	0.1
Lip	5.4	2.5
Column	1.5 - 1.7	—

Flowering period   June to February.

Distribution   Arntully, the Cockpit Country, Mason River Savanna, Hollymount and the St Andrew hills in Jamaica. Also found in Florida, from Mexico to Colombia, the Bahamas and other Caribbean islands.

Cultural notes   This plant is suitable for slab or pot culture. It is easily established, but cooler temperatures are beneficial. Keep in shaded area.

Hybridization   This plant has been crossed with other epidendrums and cattleyas.

Epidendrum
nocturnum var. latifolium

Description   *Epidendrum nocturnum* var. *latifolium* is an epiphytic plant which consists of a cluster of flattened, jointed stems up to 60 cm tall, arising from a shortened rhizome which has numerous thick roots. The stems are rounded at the base and the internodes are covered by the tubular sheathing bases of the leaves. The leaves are borne in two rows on the stems and are elliptic-lanceolate, leathery, dark green and notched at the apices. They are up to 7.5 cm long and 3.2 cm wide.

The inflorescence is terminal, the peduncle being up to 5 cm long, bearing a solitary flower. The sepals are elliptic-lanceolate, tan on the abaxial surfaces and yellowish-green on the adaxial surfaces. The petals are lanceolate and yellowish-green. The lip is white and has a narrow basal isthmus fused to the underside of the column. It has a narrow elongated midlobe about 2.5 cm long, flanked by two broader lobes which are about 8 mm wide and two upright, triangular yellow calli at the base (cf. *E. nocturnum*).

	Length (cm)	Width (cm)
Median sepal	3.8	0.65
Lateral sepal	2.8	0.62
Petal	4.3	0.3
Lip	3.4	1.8
Column	1.5	–

Flowering period September to November.

Distribution Hardwar Gap and Foxes' Gap in Jamaica. Also found in other Caribbean islands, Venezuela, Guyana and Brazil.

Cultural notes Same as for *E. nocturnum*, except that a top dressing of sphagnum moss may be necessary in hot climates since the plant is found above 1000 m (3000 ft) in Jamaica.

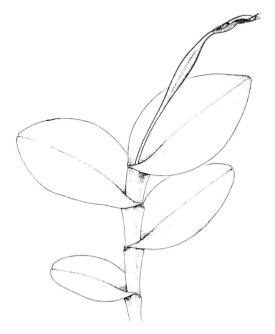

Epidendrum nutans

Description *Epidendrum nutans* is an epiphytic or lithophytic reed-type epidendrum with older stems becoming hardened, longitudinally grooved canes. The stems bear leathery, light green, linear-ovate leaves up to 19 cm long and 5 cm wide in an alternate arrangement and are sheathed by tubular leaf bases which are on average 5 cm long. The terminal inflorescence is a pendent raceme, the peduncle being up to 20 cm long with a sheathing basal bract 4.5 cm long. The pedicels are pale green and vary in length between 2.5 and 2.8 cm.

The flowers are fragrant, star-shaped, waxy, pendulous and pale green with a white lip. They are about 4.3 cm long and 4 cm wide. The median sepals are linear. The column is 7 mm long and fused to the narrow basal isthmus of the lip which juts forwards from the central axis of the flower. The base of the column is green, the anterior portion being white or cream like the limb of the lip.

The limb of the lip is convex on the upper surface, four-lobed with two rounded lobes flanking two minute pointed anterior lobes. There are two prominent crests below the aperture of the column and four small ridges extending along the midline of the lip to the apex. The size of the flower is variable.

	Length (cm)	Width (cm)
Median sepal	2.1	0.6
Lateral sepal	1.6 - 1.8	0.5 - 0.6
Petal	1.6 - 2.0	0.4
Lip	2.3	1.5
Column	1.3	1.0

Flowering period   August to March.

Distribution   Endemic. Arntully, Central Highlands, the Cockpit Country, Hardwar Gap and Hollymount.

Cultural notes   Because of its large size, the plant grows better in baskets than on tree-fern slabs. The central core of the tree-fern stem is also useful for the cultivation of this plant. Keep shaded.

Hybridization   This species has been little used in hybridization but a cross with *E. pseudepidendrum* made *E.* Jean.

Epidendrum ramosum

Description   *Epidendrum ramosum* is epiphytic with branched, trailing stems about 1m long and is anchored to the support plant by basal roots.   The shoots arise at regular intervals along the stem. The leaves are stiff, linear, notched at the apex, dark glossy green on the adaxial surface, 5 - 11 cm long with sheathing leaf bases between 2.5 - 3 mm long and 7 - 8 mm wide. The internodes are covered by the old, dessicated, tubular leaf bases.

The inflorescence is terminal and bears two or three inconspicuous green flowers. The peduncle is jointed and the lower internode and the pedicels are completely sheathed by yellowish-green bracts. The sepals are linear-lanceolate, the median sepal inclining towards the column and the lateral sepals flanking the lip.

The petals are linear, narrow and spread out horizontally. The lip is saggitate with a narrow basal isthmus closely appressed to the lateral lobes of the column. There are two raised triangular calli at the base of the limb of the lip. The column lies flat against the isthmus of the lip and is laterally compressed.

	Length (cm)	Width (cm)
Median sepal	0.6	0.15
Lateral sepal	0.6	0.2
Petal	0.5	0.05
Lip	0.6	0.3
Column	0.25	–

Flowering period August to March.

Distribution Hardwar Gap, Foxes' Gap, Morse's Gap, Hollymount and Arntully in Jamaica. Also found elsewhere in the West Indies and from Mexico to Brazil.

Cultural notes The plant may be cultivated in a medium of tree fern in a wire basket or clay pot under well shaded conditions.

Epidendrum rigidum

Description *Epidendrum rigidum* is an epiphytic plant with a narrow creeping rhizome, the short internodes of which are sheathed by scale leaves. The upright stems are covered by the sheathing bases of the leaves which are on average 2.5 cm long. The leaves are obtuse, thick, succulent, keeled along the midrib and 5 cm long and 2 cm wide.

The inflorescence is a spike up to 12.5 cm long with a zigzag form. The flowers are pale green, inconspicuous and are retained after the capsules have set. The lip is minute and fused to the column. The petals and sepals are minute, the dorsal sepal and lip incline towards each other giving the flower a closed look.

	Length (cm)	Width (cm)
Median sepal	0.5	0.28
Lateral sepal	0.6	0.2
Petal	0.5	less than 0.1
Lip	0.7	–
Column	0.3	–

Flowering period Year-round.

Distribution Fairly widespread throughout the island. Also found in Florida, the Bahamas and other Caribbean islands and from Mexico to South America.

Cultural notes Culture on tree-fern slabs is best because of the creeping habit of the plant. Lightly shaded conditions are necessary.

Epidendrum rivulare

Description *Epidendrum rivulare* is an epiphytic plant with pendent branches sprouting from a common rhizome bearing a cluster of thick, white glabrous roots. The stems are pale green, up to 85 cm long, the apex of each terminating in an inflorescence in the mature plant. The leaves are lanceolate, dark glossy green, up to 13.5 cm long and 1.3 cm wide. The peduncle is up to 12 cm long and is covered by flattened, stiff, apiculate overlapping bracts which are up to 5.6 cm long.

The inflorescence is few-flowered, the flowers being non-resupinate and star-shaped. The pedicels are up to 2.6 cm long. The sepals are thick, linear-lanceolate, and the petals linear. Both the petals and sepals are greenish-cream and patterned with reddish-purple spots on the adaxial surfaces.

The cream-coloured lip has a narrow basal isthmus which is fused to the under surface of the column and expands anteriorly into a trilobed limb having a fimbriate margin. There are two small calli on the limb of the lip near the apex of the column and a few reddish spots on the adaxial surface.

	Length (cm)	Width (cm)
Median sepal	1.6 - 1.8	0.5 - 0.6
Lateral sepal	1.7	0.6
Petal	1.5 - 1.65	0.1
Lip	1.3 - 1.5	1.0
Column	0.7	0.3

Flowering period August to March.

Distribution Hollymount, Green River, Glenwood Springs, between Balcarres and Sunbury, Quaco Rock, Boothe District, Douglas Castle, Woodstock, Johnson Mountain and Bamboo in Jamaica. Also found in Cuba and Hispaniola.

Cultural notes The plant adapts well to slab or basket culture. Keep in a cool, well-shaded area.

Epidendrum tomlinsonianum

Description *Epidendrum tomlinsonianum* has tall leafy shoots up to 90 cm high and sometimes higher, bearing leathery lanceolate leaves 16 - 20 cm long and about 4 cm wide. The inflorescence is a pendulous raceme arising from a terminal leaf axil, bearing about eighteen flowers, the peduncle being covered with overlapping bracts for most of its length which can be up to 23.5 cm.

The flowers are small and green with purple spots on the lip. The pedicels are light green as are the sepals and petals, but the latter are marked with purple veins. The median sepal is ovate and overhangs the column which projects forward from the axis of the flower; the shiny lateral sepals are paired and elliptical with sharply pointed apices curving under the auricles of the lip.

The petals are linear, very narrow, 1.2 mm wide, elliptical and curving antrorsely. The foot of the column is narrow, green and expands anteriorly into two flattened side lobes, the undersides of the foot and lobes being fused to the narrow basal isthmus of the lip to form a tube. The limb of the lip is convex on the upper surface. It has two lateral auricles, each flanking the crest which marks the midline of the lip and two small pointed anterior lobes. The lip has two small purple calli, one on either side of the aperture of the tube. There are two purple kidney-shaped blotches, one on either side of the crest.

	Length (cm)	Width (cm)
Median sepal	1.2 - 1.4	0.6
Lateral sepal	1.2 - 1.4	0.5
Petal	1.2 - 1.3	0.1 - 0.2
Lip	1.5	1.3
Column	0.9	–

Flowering period January to June.

Distribution Endemic. Lluidas Vale, Manchester, Arntully, the Cockpit Country and Hollymount.

Cultural notes As for *E. nutans*.

Epidendrum tomlinsonianum x nutans

Description   *Epidendrum tomlinsonianum* x *nutans* is an epiphytic plant which has stout leafy shoots up to 80 cm tall. The leaves are linear, notched at the apices, up to 21.8 cm long and 6.3 cm wide. The inflorescence is a raceme up to 29 cm long, bearing up to about thirty flowers on pedicels about 2.2 cm long on average. The sepals and petals all lie in the same plane; they are thick, elliptic and waxy-green tipped with purple. The petals are narrower than the sepals.

The lip has a narrow basal isthmus about 0.7 cm long which is fused to the underside of the column, leaving a narrow opening at the front. It is greenish-cream and expands anteriorly into a four-lobed limb which has a narrow median callus flanked by two amethyst blotches.

	Length (cm)	Width (cm)
Median sepal	1.3	0.6
Lateral sepal	1.2 - 1.4	0.5 - 0.6
Petal	1.1 - 1.3	0.3
Lip	1.2 - 1.7	1.3 - 1.4
Column	0.8	—

Flowering period March to April.

Distribution Endemic. Banana Ground and Auchtembeddie.

Cultural notes Same as for *E. nutans*.

The main difference between this plant and its parents is that *E. nutans* has flowers which are well displayed and discrete. *E. tomlinsonianum* has flowers which resemble a bunch of grapes on a much shorter unbranched peduncle. The hybrid has flowers which are intermediate.

Epidendrum verrucosum

Description *Epidendrum verrucosum* is one of the larger epidendrums which is sometimes found on trees but is mostly terrestrial or lithophytic. The plant consists of a group of cylindrical stems from which arise a bundle of thick, white, glabrous roots. The stems are up to 2.5 m tall, with internodes about 3.5 cm long, covered by the tubular bases of the leaves which have numerous dark brown warts. The leaves appear in two ranks along the stem with the leaf blades curving downwards at the apices; they are dark green, lanceolate, up to 21.5 cm long and 4.5 - 5 cm wide.

The inflorescence is a large, many-branched panicle up to 56 cm tall, bearing numerous small, fragrant, green and white flowers. The sepals and petals are pale green; the sepals are ovate and slightly concave at the tips. The petals are linear-ligulate, spreading outwards on either side of the column. The lip is white and has a narrow basal isthmus which is fused to the lateral lobes of the column to form a funnel-shaped tube. There is a three-ridged yellow callus at the entrance of the tube. The limb of the lip is trilobed with the mid-lobe bifurcating near the centre and projecting downwards. The column is white with a green base, its upper margin deeply toothed, forming a hooded fringe above the anther. The anther cap is green.

	Length (cm)	Width (cm)
Median sepal	0.6 - 0.7	0.4
Lateral sepal	0.6 - 0.7	0.35
Petal	0.55	0.15
Lip	0.9 - 1.1	0.9 - 1.0
Column	0.5	0.3

Flowering period   November to March.

Distribution   Widespread in areas over 680 m (2000 ft) in St Andrew and St Thomas in Jamaica. Also found in Cuba and from Mexico to Colombia.

Cultural notes   The plant should be potted in tree fern or charcoal and placed in a well illuminated area.

Hybridization   This species has been little used in hybridization, but it has been crossed with other epidendrums and with *Schombolaelia Colorful* to form *Dillonara San Antonio*.

ERYTHRODES

From the Greek *erythrodes*, reddish;
from the floral colour of some species.

Erythrodes hirtella

Description *Erythrodes hirtella* is a terrestrial plant up to
40 cm tall when in bloom. The plant has soft, pale green,
trailing stems each ending in a scape, with stout roots arising
from the lower nodes. The leaves are spirally arranged in a
cluster, they are elliptic-lanceolate, apiculate, petiolate, have
sheathing bases and are up to 5 cm long and 2.7 cm wide. Both
the petioles and the sheathing leaf-bases of the leaves are very
pale green. The scape is pale green, pubescent and bears
several flowers in a spike.

The sepals and petals are pale green; the sepals are translucent and hairy on the abaxial surfaces. The median sepal is
ligulate and concave at the base; the lateral sepals are arcuate
and rounded and incurved at the apices, overlap the lateral
lobes of the lip and are closely appressed to the sides of the
median sepal.

The lip enfolds the column; it is trough-shaped, fleshy and
pale green on the lower half where it is extended into a short
green spur. The lip is white and recurved at the margin, with
two minute ear-like lobes on either side of a broad median lobe.

	Length (cm)	Width (cm)
Median sepal	0.25 - 0.5	0.1
Lateral sepal	0.2 - 0.6	0.1
Petal	0.3 - 0.5	0.1
Lip	0.35 - 0.6	0.2 - 0.3
Column	0.1 - 0.3	0 - 0.5

Flowering period January to April.

Distribution The Red Light District, Silver Hill Gap and the Mabess River in Jamaica. Wider distribution in Cuba, Puerto Rico, Domincia, Guadeloupe, Grenada and Trinidad.

Cultural notes Any terrestrial mix would suffice. Make sure the medium is well drained. Keep in a cool damp area.

Erythrodes plantaginea

Description *Erythrodes plantaginea* is a terrestrial plant which has upright leafy shoots up to 50 cm tall when in flower, arising from a horizontal, terete, trailing rhizome. The latter bears a single, white, thick, hairy root at each node. The leaves are light green, ovate-elliptical, pointed at the apices, have two well defined veins on either side of the midrib and undulate margins. They are 7.5 - 10 cm long and 3.2 cm wide, tapering at the base into a petiole which expands basally to form a short, tubular sheath.

The inflorescence is a raceme up to 23 cm tall. The peduncle is hairy and jointed, with short, pale green or cream bracts at each node and bears about sixteen white tubular flowers, each subtended by a cream-coloured bract. Each flower has a green, curved pedicellate ovary about 7 mm long, covered with minute hairs.

The sepals are green and pubescent on the dorsal surface. The median sepal is ovate, the lateral sepals are linear-elliptic and project forwards along the sides of the lip and petals which are translucent and elliptic-lanceolate. The lip is extended basally into a membranous, saccate spur 4.5 mm long and is trough-shaped for most of its length. The front lobe is spathulate and trilobed at the apex. The column is white and pointed.

	Length (cm)	Width (cm)
Median sepal	0.6	0.25
Lateral sepal	0.6	0.2
Petal	0.5	0.2
Lip	0.7	0.4
Spur	0.45	–
Column	0.35	–

Flowering period November to May.

Distribution The Cockpit Country, Fairy Glade, Hollymount and Lydford in Jamaica. Also found in other Caribbean islands.

Cultural notes Plant is best grown in a basket with shredded tree fern and leaf mould. A good amount of shade is required.

EULOPHIA

From the Greek *eu*, well and *lophos*,
plume or crest; from the crested lip.

Eulophia alta

Description *Eulophia alta* is terrestrial; 1 - 1.5 m tall when
in bloom. It has upright, leafy shoots each sprouting from a
flattened wedge-shaped tuber with thick, white roots growing
from the bases of the shoots. The leaves are lanceolate, plicate,
up to 90 cm long and longer and 7 cm wide. The scape is up to
80 cm long and longer, the diameter about 1 cm; it is covered
at the nodes by a few papery bracts 5.5 - 9 cm long.

   The flowers are slightly fleshy and number twenty or more
per inflorescence. The sepals and petals are light olive-green,
the sepals being linear-lanceolate, erect and spreading behind
the column and petals. The petals are oblong-ovate, overhanging the curved column and fused basally to the back of the
latter. The column is pale green and extends into a foot below
the attachment to the petals.

The lip is trilobed and hinged to the column foot forming a sac at the base; it is green and tinged with pale brownish-purple on the inner surface. The lateral lobes are erect and greenish; the median lobe has a crenulate margin and five indistinct rows of crests with two prominent papillae on the disc.

	Length (cm)	Width (cm)
Median sepal	2.1	0.6
Lateral sepal	2.6	0.7
Petal	1.5	0.75
Lip	2.3	1.4
Column	1.6	–

Flowering period May to August.

Distribution The Cockpit Country and Hollymount in Jamaica. Also found in other Caribbean islands, in West Africa, Mexico, Central America, Brazil and South Florida.

Cultural notes For greenhouse culture we recommend a mixture of fine bagasse, charcoal dust, small pieces of charcoal and tree fern, tree-fern siftings and crushed leaf mould. This mixture allows good drainage and a certain amount of moisture retention. A fair amount of light is beneficial.

EURYSTYLES

From the Greek *eurys*, broad and *stylis*, style; descriptive of the short, broad column of the type species of the genus.

Eurystyles ananassocomos

Description *Eurystyles ananassocomos* is an epiphytic plant which consists of a basal rosette of leaves which are elliptic-ovate, tapered at the base, thin, shiny, pale green and up to 2.7 cm long and 1 cm wide.

The inflorescence is axial and pendulous. The peduncle is about 3.2 cm long and bears several minute whitish flowers each subtended by an ovate buff-coloured bract which is about 9 mm long and 5 mm wide, densely hairy and keeled along the midrib. The median sepal is linear and inrolled at the margins and the lateral sepals are recurved. The petals are ovate-lanceolate, concave at the base and flank the upright column. The column is arrow-shaped at the apex. The lip is fused to the column and has three narrow anterior lobes.

	Length (cm)	Width (cm)
Median sepal	0.3	0.1
Lateral sepal	0.3	0.1
Petal	0.3	0.1
Lip	0.3	–
Column	0.3	–

Flowering period January to March.

Distribution St Andrew, St Thomas and St Ann in Jamaica. Also found in Cuba and Hispaniola.

Cultural notes A medium of leaf mould and tree-fern fibre is recommended for this species, with its thick, hairy roots. Placement in a cool shaded spot is also recommended.

GOVENIA

Named in honour of J. H. Goven, a nineteenth-century English gardener, horticulturist and plant collector in Assam.

Govenia utriculata

Description   *Govenia utriculata* is a terrestrial plant which bears two leaves arising from a corm, the long petioles supported by a large sheathing scale leaf about 20 cm long and 15 cm wide at the widest portion. This scale leaf is subtended by a much smaller one. It is soft, pale green, streaked with purple, narrow and apiculate at the top and inflated at the basal portion, so that at maturity it is filled with stored water. The corm is smooth, cream-coloured, about 4.5 cm in diameter and partially covered by the above-mentioned scale leaves. A few fibrous roots spring from its base.

The leaf blades are light green, elliptic-lanceolate, plicate and crinkled, erect, 49 cm long, and up to 12.7 cm wide. The petioles are tubular with one encircling the other; they are succulent, about 14 cm long, three-angled and green, streaked with purple. The scape arises from the side of the corm near to the leaves, within the large sheathing scale leaf; it is also green and speckled with purple, is up to 76 cm tall and jointed with tubular pale green sheaths covering the internodes.

About thirty flowers are borne near the upper end of the scape, each subtended by a pale green bract. The flowers open partially, the paired lateral sepals being arcuate with the apices almost touching, and project outwards. The median sepal is linear-lanceolate and overlaps the paired petals which shield the column; the petals are white with pale amethyst barring, arcuate with the apices divaricate.

The lip is ovate with a short claw articulating with the column foot; it is erect and curved being closely appressed to the column, the apex lying free. The lip has two indistinct pale yellow calli and the apex is marked with three small purple spots. The column is concave and barred with amethyst on the adaxial surface, it has two lateral lobes on the upper half and is extended into a short column foot. The ovary is pedicellate.

	Length (cm)	Width (cm)
Median sepal	2.2	0.5
Lateral sepal	1.3	0.5
Petal	1.7	0.8
Lip	1.0	0.6
Column	0.9	0.6

Flowering period   September to April.

Distribution   Arntully, Hollymount and the Tobolski Mines in Jamaica. Also found in Mexico, through Central America to Argentina, the Bahamas and the Greater Antilles.

Cultural notes   This plant should be potted in a mixture of leaf mould and charcoal fines or any other terrestrial mix and kept well shaded.

HABENARIA

From *habens*, reins; referring to the elongated, strap-like division of the petals and lip.

Habenaria jamaicensis

Description *Habenaria jamaicensis* is a terrestrial plant which has mostly basal leaves arranged in a spiral on a central stem arising from a swollen rhizome. The plant is up to 30 cm tall when in flower. The leaves are soft, pale shiny green and elliptic-lanceolate.

The inflorescence is a terminal raceme which bears about ten green flowers. The sepals are pale green and three-nerved; the median sepal is cucullate and the lateral sepals arcuate. The petals are lobed at the base, yellowish-green, arcuate, upright and flank the median sepal.

The lip is yellowish-green, elongated into a spur 1.5 cm long at the base and divided into three filamentous lobes, the lateral lobes being longer than the median and up to 1.1 cm long. The median lobe is 7 mm long. The column is very short, erect with anther cells on either side. The pollinia are stalked, each ending in a round gland. The stigma has two rounded protuberances.

	Length (cm)	Width (cm)
Median sepal	0.7	0.5
Lateral sepal	0.6	0.2
Petal	0.6	0.1
Lip	1.1	–
Column	0.3	–

Flowering period December to April.

Distribution Near Guava Ridge. Also found in Guatemala and Hispaniola.

Cultural notes Plant in a terrestrial mix and keep in a cool, well-shaded area.

Habenaria monorrhiza

Description *Habenaria monorrhiza* is a terrestrial plant which grows in colonies, each stem having an upright stem that terminates in a many-flowered raceme. The roots are bundled together and have one main tuber. The plants in flower are up to 93 cm tall. The leaves are greyish-green, spirally arranged, keeled with tubular sheathing bases speckled with dark brown; they are stiff, ovate-lanceolate, have thin white margins, three prominent veins, and are about 11.4 cm long and 4 - 4.5 cm wide.

The flowers are white and have green, twisted, winged, pedicellate ovaries about 1.7 cm long. The sepals are ovate and concave, the median sepal hooded, the lateral sepals arcuate. The petals are elliptic sometimes with a fine anterior filament attached to each. The lip has one median lobe 6 - 7 mm long and two filamentous lateral lobes. The base is protracted into a spur 2.1 - 2.5 cm long with two small crests appearing at the orifice.

	Length (cm)	Width (cm)
Median sepal	0.7	0.6
Lateral sepal	0.9	0.45
Petal	0.7	0.2
Lip	0.75	–
Spur	1.3 - 2.0	

Flowering period October to April.

Distribution Found on rocky hillsides and bank sides at Knockpatrick, the Red Light District and Silver Hill Gap in Jamaica. Also found in other Caribbean islands and from Guatemala to Peru and Brazil.

Cultural notes The same as for *Govenia utriculata*. A fair amount of light should be given to these plants. They die back after blooming and remain dormant until the next growing season.

Habenaria quinqueseta

(macroceratitis)

Description *Habenaria quinqueseta* is terrestrial with a small irregular tuber found at the ends of the brittle white roots which emerge from the base of the stem. The average height of flowering plants varies according to the colony in which they are found and ranges from 60 - 90 cm. The aerial part of the plant consists of an erect, succulent stem which terminates in a racemose inflorescence. The leaves are ovate-elliptic, pliant, pale green with tubular bases; they diminish in size towards the apex and the base, those of the middle portion being up to 13.5 cm long and longer, and 4.1 cm wide, those at the apex appearing bract-like.

The flowers are spirally arranged around the terminal portion of the stem; the sepals are pale green, the median sepal ovate, forming a cockle-shaped hood with the upper lobes of the petals above the column. The lateral sepals are arcuate when spread flat, but are folded backwards at the base and obliquely along their upper halves. The petals are white and bilobed, the upper lobes being arcuate and closely appressed to the margins of the median sepal; the lower lobes are filiform, spreading outwards and curling at their ends.

The lip is white, trilobed, the median lobe revolute and about 1.8 cm long; the lateral lobes filiform and 5 - 5.5 cm long. The lip is united with the column basally and extended into a flattened green spur up to 12 cm long. The column is complex with a thin membranous shielding portion behind the stigma, having two slits at the sides which enclose a pair of pollinia; the caudicles are thin and threadlike, the viscidia are found in two papillae. The stigma consists of two flattened lobes, sticky on the upper surface, which encircle the aperture and meet in front at the centre of the aperture of the spur and merge at the back to form a triangular flap of tissue which is connivent with the shield-like portion of the column.

	Length (cm)	Width (cm)
Median sepal	1.4	1.1
Lateral sepal	1.5	0.8
Upper lobe of petal	1.3	0.35
Lower lobe of petal	3.7	0.15
Lateral lobe of lip	4.8	0.15
Median lobe of lip	1.8	0.25
Column	0.4	0.4
Spur	10.0 - 12.0	–

Flowering period October to January.

Distribution High altitude savannas and grass lands, rocky hillsides and banks in Jamaica. Also found in the south- eastern United States to northern South America, Cuba and Hispaniola.

Cultural notes Same as for *Govenia utriculata*.

HARRISELLA

Dedicated to William Harris, former Superintendent of Public Gardens in Jamaica and an indefatigable plant collector.

Harrisella porrecta

Description *Harrisella porrecta* is a miniature, leafless, epiphytic plant with glabrous, greenish roots radiating from a short central stem, some of which adhere to the bark of the support plant by running lengthwise along the stem. The scape is thin, zigzagged, up to 3.7 cm long, and bears about six flowers in succession.

The flowers are golden yellow, minute, translucent and borne on pedicels about 3 mm long. The sepals are ovate-elliptic and overlap the petals at the base, curving outwards.

The cockle-shaped lip has a small apiculus and at the base there is a globular, transparent green sac curving towards the median sepal, thereby enclosing the flattened column.

	Length (cm)	Width (cm)
Median sepal	0.2	0.25
Lateral sepal	0.2	0.1
Petal	0.35	0.1
Lip	0.3	0.3
Spur	0.07	–

Flowering period   October to November.

Distribution   Hope River valley and the Mammee River valley in St Andrew, Jamaica. Also found in Florida, Mexico, El Salvador, Cuba and Hispaniola.

Cultural notes   The plant grows well in cultivation when left on the twig on which it was found and placed in a well lit area.

HOMALOPETALUM

From the Greek *homalos*, even or uniform and *petalon*, petal; from the similar perianth segments.

Homalopetalum vomeriforme

Description   *Homalopetalum vomeriforme* is a tiny epiphyte with unifoliate, wedge-shaped pseudobulbs, each about 4 - 6 mm tall, arising alternately on a very slender rhizome. The old portion of the plant adheres to the support plant, while younger, apical portions grow freely, without attachment. The leaves are ovate, fleshy, up to 1.5 cm long, the older leaves about 7 mm wide, the younger ones being narrower.

The inflorescence arises from the axil of the leaf at the apex of the pseudobulb. The peduncles are filiform and about 2.2 cm long; the older leafless pseudobulbs retain the dried peduncles.

The sepals and petals are membranous and buff-coloured with a tinge of pink. The sepals are acuminate, recurved at their tips, the median sepal is lanceolate and the lateral sepals arcuate; the petals are acuminate and arcuate.

The lip is sagittate, yellowish and has fine veins; the lateral lobes of the former overlap to form a tube anterior to the column which is erect, slender and green.

	Length (cm)	Width (cm)
Median sepal	1.2 - 1.5	0.2 - 0.3
Lateral sepal	1.2 - 1.5	0.1 - 0.3
Petal	1.2 - 1.6	0.1 - 0.4
Lip	1.3 - 1.7	0.1 - 0.6
Column	0.5	0.1

Flowering period   October to January.

Distribution   Arntully, Hollymount and the Red Light District in Jamaica. Also found in Cuba.

Cultural notes   It is best to use a small thumb pot to grow this plant but a small tree-fern slab could also be used. A medium of shredded tree-fern could also be used for potting. Keep well shaded. This plant is usually found growing downwards.

IONOPSIS

From the Greek *ion*, violet
and *opsis*, appearing; from
the fancied resemblance of
these flowers to violets.

Ionopsis satyrioides

Description *Ionopsis satyrioides* is epiphytic and has six or seven terete leaves between 12.5 and 13 cm long in larger specimens and 3.2 mm wide, arising from a short stem. The leaves are often deeply reddish-purple when exposed to full sunlight. The roots are fine and white. The axillary inflorescence is a panicle up to 20 cm long and longer.

The flowers are minute, creamy-white, fragrant of citron, with the petals and sepals overlapping at their bases and spreading above the lip to form a fringe. The sepals are ovate-apiculate and concave at their bases. The petals are oblong-ovate with fine violet-coloured nerves, the margins slightly undulate. The lip is pandurate (fiddle-shaped) and bilobed. The column is grey-green and has a foot which forms a mentum with the lip. The ovary is pedicellate.

	Length (cm)	Width (cm)
Median sepal	0.7	0.3
Lateral sepal	0.7	0.2
Petal	0.7	0.3
Lip	1.1	0.5
Column	0.3	—

Flowering period   Year-round.

Distribution   Portland, Moneague, Ramble (St Ann), Ramble (St Elizabeth), Golden Spring and Manchester in Jamaica. Also found in Hispaniola, Puerto Rico, Trinidad and Venezuela.

Cultural notes   This plant grows best when attached to a twig, as found in nature, under dry atmospheric conditions and bright light.

Ionopsis utricularioides

Description   *Ionopsis utricularioides* is epiphytic with shoots arising from a rhizome, each shoot bearing a bundle of fine white roots basally. Some roots are exserted through the old leaf bases, a characteristic it shares with equitant oncidiums.

The leaves are linear-lanceolate, leathery and stiff, with prominent ridges on their upper surfaces, up to 16 cm long and 1.3 cm wide. They vary from light to dark green, are paired and overlap at their bases around a small leafless pseudobulb. The latter is flat, linear-ovate, slightly ribbed and up to 1.6 cm long and 3 mm wide.

The inflorescence is a panicle arising from the base of the pseudobulb with the peduncle sometimes attaining a length of up to 60 cm. The flowers, borne on pale green pedicels 9 mm long, are very pale mauve or pinkish with violet veins on the lip, median sepal and petals. An alba form of the species is known.

The lateral sepals are elliptic and extend basally into a short spur; the median sepal and petals are ovate with violet veins and these form a short fringe above the base of the lip. The lip is predominant, flares outwards from the base into two equal notched lobes and has two small yellow crests on the disc. The column is minute and pale green.

	Length (cm)	Width (cm)
Median sepal	0.4 - 0.5	0.2 - 0.3
Lateral sepal	0.5	0.2
Petal	0.6	0.25 - 0.3
Lip	1.1 - 1.2	1.4
Column	0.2	—

Flowering period Year-round with a peak from June to October.

Distribution Widespread throughout the island on *Ficus*, guava, citrus and calabash trees. Also found in Florida, from Mexico to Venezuela, the Lesser Antilles and Grand Cayman.

Cultural notes Plant adapts well to slab or basket culture using charcoal. Keep well illuminated.

Hybridization This species has been crossed with rodrettias and also with *Comparettia* to give *Ionettia*.

Ionopsis utricularioides x satyrioides

Description *Ionopsis utricularioides* x *satyrioides* is an epiphytic plant with shoots consisting of two or three leaves overlapping at their bases and protected by scarious sheaths. Long glabrous roots arise from the bases of the shoots. A short, flattened pseudobulb, about 1.5 cm long, is present in the axil of the innermost leaves. The leaves are stiff, lanceolate, apiculate, thick, light green and deeply furrowed on the adaxial surface; they have overlapping petioles and are up to 12.2 cm long and 1.3 cm wide.

The axial inflorescence is a peduncle up to 27.5 cm long, the pedicels being less than 1 cm long. The floral segments are pale lavender, thin and patterned with linear, purple nerves. The median sepal is ovate-lanceolate, the lateral sepals lanceolate and connate for one third of their length, forming a chin at the base of the flower but spreading widely at their apices. The petals are oblong and rounded at the apices. The lip is flared into two rounded anterior lobes which are notched on the margins and tapered at the base to form a narrow isthmus which has a cream-coloured median band flanked by two linear yellow calli.

	Length (cm)	Width (cm)
Median sepal	0.5 - 0.7	0.2
Lateral sepal	0.5 - 0.7	0.2
Petal	0.6	0.2 - 0.25
Lip	1.2 - 1.3	0.8 - 1.0
Column	0.15	0.1

Flowering period March to July.

Distribution Darliston and the north Cockpit Country in Jamaica.

Cultural notes Same as for *I. utricularioides* and *I. satyrioides*.

NB The leaves of *I. utricularioides* are strongly ribbed but those of *I. satyrioides* are terete. The strongly keeled, smooth leaves of the hybrid *I. satyrioides x utricularioides* are intermediate. Dimensions of the floral segments of the hybrid are similar to those of *I. utricularioides*, except for the width of the lip.

ISOCHILUS

From the Greek *isos*, equal and *cheilos*, lip; probably because of the equality in size between the lip and sepals.

Isochilus linearis

Description *Isochilus linearis* is a lithophytic or epiphytic plant consisting of leafy, spreading shoots with thin stems arising from a short rhizome. Thick white roots sprout at intervals from the latter. The leaves are narrow, linear with overlapping bases, up to 5.2 cm long and 5 mm wide and are arranged pinnately on the stems.

The inflorescence is a curved, one-sided raceme; the peduncle is an extension of the stem apex about 4 cm long. The flowers are amethyst, tubular, non-resupinate, each borne on a pedicel about 0.5 mm long and held in an upright position; numbering about seven or eight per raceme. The sepals are linear-lanceolate, folded along the median line, and enclose the petals and the lip; the lateral sepals are saccate at the base.

The lip is lavender, ligulate and abruptly depressed in the middle where it has two triangular amethyst spots; it is narrowed at the base and articulates with the column foot. The column is whitish with two apical lavender lobes at the sides and has a short foot.

	Length (cm)	Width (cm)
Median sepal	0.8	0.7
Lateral sepal	1.0	0.3
Petal	0.6	0.3
Lip	0.8	0.25
Column	0.5	–

Flowering period   At various times throughout the year.

Distribution   Arntully, Clydesdale, the Cockpit Country, Manchester and Hollymount in Jamaica. Also found in Mexico and from Cuba to Argentina.

Cultural notes   The plant is best grown in a basket with a mixture of tree fern, charcoal and sphagnum moss in medium shade.

JACQUINIELLA

Dedicated to the eighteenth/nineteenth century Dutch-born Austrian botanist Nikolas Joseph von Jacquin, who visited the Caribbean islands and mainland. He later published extensively on the plants he found while a professor in Vienna.

Jacquiniella globosa

Description *Jacquiniella globosa* is an epiphytic plant up to 15 cm tall, having slender, flattened, jointed stems growing together in tufts. The leaves are almost terete, grooved, leathery, bright green, up to 1.6 cm long and 1.5 mm wide. The flowers are borne in groups of two or three on pedicels measuring 2 - 3 mm at the tops of the shoots.

The sepals are cucullate, ovate, translucent, tinged with purple and connate for almost half their length forming a tube at the base. The petals are elliptic, pale green, translucent and adnate to the sepals. The lip is pale green, scoop-shaped with rounded lateral lobes, and has a short spur at the base where it is adnate to the lateral sepals; there is an apiculus flanked by the lateral lobes of the lip. The column is pale green. The fruits are globose with six segments.

	Length (cm)	Width (cm)
Median sepal	0.25 - 0.5	0.1
Lateral sepal	0.25 - 0.5	0.1
Petal	0.3	0.1
Lip	0.3	0.2
Column	0.2 - 0.3	0.1 - 0.15

Flowering period Sporadically throughout the year.

Distribution Highlands of Jamaica, Central America, the Greater Antilles, Guadeloupe and Colombia.

Cultural notes Plants should be grown in the shade and in a humid and cool atmosphere. They thrive on twigs or in small pots with either gravel or sphagnum moss.

Jacquiniella teretifolia

Description *Jacquiniella teretifolia* is an epiphytic plant with erect clustered shoots arising from a short rhizome. The stems are up to 30 cm tall, yellowish, flattened, swollen at the bases and sheathed along the internodes by the leaf bases. The leaves are terete with a groove on the adaxial surface and are about 3.2 cm long. In fertile shoots the uppermost internode is elongated to about 5 cm and bears a terminal leaf at the apex, in the axil of which a solitary green flower is borne.

The peduncle is about 5 mm long. The sepals are linear-lanceolate, stiff and erect, shielding the petals and the lip. The petals are spathulate, the lip linear-lanceolate with erect lateral lobes. The column is erect, lobed at the apex and fused with the lip for about half of its length at the base to form a narrow tube.

	Length (cm)	Width (cm)
Median sepal	0.8	0.3
Lateral sepal	1.1	0.2
Petal	0.5	1.5
Lip	0.6 - 0.8	–
Column	0.2 - 0.4	–

Flowering period   October to December.

Distribution   Upper Swift River and Fairy Glade, Foxes' Gap and Hollymount in Jamaica; other Caribbean islands and from Mexico to Panama, Venezuela and Colombia.

Cultural notes   The plant is quite hardy and does well in cultivation. It must be grown in the shade and in a humid atmosphere. A mixture of tree fern and charcoal or stones and a top dressing of sphagnum moss is adequate for pot culture.

LEOCHILUS

From the Greek *leios*, smooth and *cheilos*, lip; referring to the smooth lip.

Leochilus labiatus

Description *Leochilus labiatus* is one of the truly delightful miniature epiphytic orchids. The plant has small, flattened, rounded pseudobulbs 1.3 cm tall and 1.1 cm wide, sheathed by the bases of a pair of ovate leaves and bearing a solitary leaf at the apices. The leaves are 5 cm long and 1.3 cm wide, crisp, slightly leathery and green on the (upper) adaxial surface.

The inflorescences arise from the bases of the pseudobulbs, sometimes in pairs one on either side, sometimes singly. The peduncle, which may be up to 24 cm long, is sometimes pendent and bears six or seven flowers. The flowers do not open fully; the median sepal and petals overlap each other and project forwards over the column. The petals and sepals have a red-dish-brown background and two rows of yellow blotches. The column is yellow. The lip is ovate and has two reddish-brown blotches at its base.

	Length (cm)	Width (cm)
Median	0.5	0.2
Lateral sepal	0.6	0.2
Petal	0.6	0.2
Lip	0.6	0.35
Column	0.15	–

Flowering period Year-round.

Distribution Fairly widespread throughout the island. Also found from Honduras to Panama, Venezuela and other Caribbean islands.

Cultural notes Culture on tree fern slabs or pieces of citrus; calabash is best because of the creeping habit of the plant. *Leochilus labiatus* should be exposed to strong light.

Hybridization This plant has been little used but has been hybridized with *Oncidium onustum*, *O. pulchellum* and *O. triquetrum*.

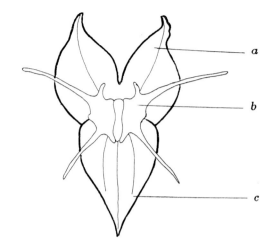

LEPANTHES

From the Greek *lepis*, scale and *anthos*, flower; because of the minute, scale-like flowers of many species.

Lepanthes cochlearifolia

Description   *Lepanthes cochlearifolia* is an epiphytic plant with unifoliate stems up to 4 cm long radiating from a central rhizome. The internodes of the stems are covered by ridged sheaths which have setae on the margins of their widely dilated mouths and ridges. The leaves are elliptical or orbicular, mucronate, green on the adaxial surface and sometimes purple underneath; they are up to 2.4 cm long and 2 cm wide.

The inflorescences are borne in groups of two to four in the axils of the leaves. The peduncles are up to 8 mm long. The flowers are reddish. The sepals are reddish violet, the lateral sepals being joined together for one-third of their length, each having a pair of nerves. The median sepal has a long median nerve flanked by two shorter ones. The petals are very small, their width being almost equal to the width of one of the lateral sepals. They are bright orange, clawed, with blunt anterior lobes and apiculate posterior lobes.

The lip is deep crimson, axe-shaped with the anterior lobes tapering into a pair of horn-like processes; it is adnate to the column near the apex of the latter.

	Length (cm)	Width (cm)
Median sepal	0.5	0.2
Lateral sepal	0.5	0.2
Petal	0.1	1.5
Lip	1.5	2.0
Column	0.1	–
Flower	0.9	0.5

Flowering period   July to August and November to April.

Distribution   Endemic. Found in Hollymount, Hardwar Gap and Foxes' Gap.

Cultural notes   Plant in a small plastic or clay pot in a mixture of charcoal and tree-fern fibre, or on a twig with coir or sphagnum moss as backing material. Keep in a cool, well lit but not sunny area.

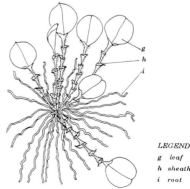

LEGEND
g   leaf
h   sheath
i   root

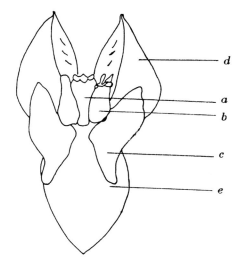

Lepanthes divaricata

Description *Lepanthes divaricata* is epiphytic and grows in tufts, the very fine roots embedded in the moss and anchoring it to the trunks of supporting trees. It has very slender jointed unifoliate stems, 4 - 18 cm tall, the internodes covered by tubular sheaths which have finely tapered apices, their margins and veins having minute hairs.

The leaves are solitary, leathery, apiculate, elliptic, pale or dark green with a concentration of purple pigment on the abaxial surfaces of the veins and in the petioles; they are up to 5.2 cm long and 2.8 cm wide. Several racemes each about 3.6 cm long, arise from the axil of the leaf, subtended by a sheath, each developing in sequence.

Only one or two flowers open at a time. The sepals are ovate, pale yellow and translucent; the lateral sepals are connate for about one-third of their length, their apices divaricate, each having a central vein demarcating an inner darker segment. The petals are vermilion, roughly triangular anteriorly, each with a triangular lobe pointing towards the centre and tapering into a narrow posterior lobe which is sometimes tinged with yellow. The lip is about half the length of the petals and is divided at the centre into two pear-shaped, orange-red lateral lobes which embrace the column. The column is cerise and bears two yellow pollinia.

	Length (cm)	Width (cm)
Median sepal	0.3	0.2
Lateral sepal	0.2	0.15
Petal	0.3	0.1
Flower	0.5	0.3

Flowering period   Most of the year.

Distribution   Endemic. St Andrew, Portland and St Thomas.

Cultural notes   Same as for *L. cochlearifolia*.

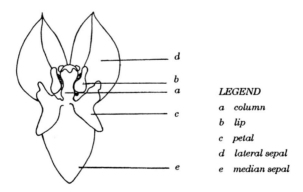

LEGEND

a   column
b   lip
c   petal
d   lateral sepal
e   median sepal

Lepanthes elliptica

Description *Lepanthes elliptica* is a plant which has a cluster of unifoliate stems up to 11 cm long which are covered by tubular sheaths on the internodes; the mouths of the sheaths are non-dilated, apiculate and the ridges are smooth. The leaves are stiff, leathery, bright green, broadly elliptical and up to 3 cm long and 2.4 cm wide. The sepals are golden yellow, ovate, the lateral sepals being connate for half their length, the tips divaricate and tinged with crimson. The petals are unequally lobed, deltate, the posterior tapering to an acute point. The lip is trilobed, with two large peltate lobes embracing the column with a median apiculus lying behind the column; the lip is orange, tinged with crimson and the column is crimson and club-shaped.

	Length (cm)	Width (cm)
Flower	0.6	0.3
Median sepal	0.25	0.2
Lateral sepal	0.25	0.15
Petal	0.1	0.2
Lip	0.1	0.15
Column	0.1	0.05

Flowering period January to April.

Distribution Endemic. Hollymount and Mount Diablo.

Cultural notes This plant does well on a small twig, placing either sphagnum moss or coir fibre between the plant and the twig. Keep in a fairly open area, about 45 per cent shade.

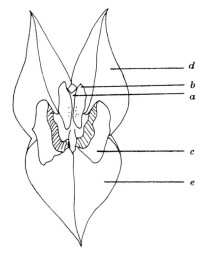

Lepanthes intermedia

Description *Lepanthes intermedia* is an epiphytic plant which consists of a tuft of unifoliate stems 7.5 - 8.8 cm tall arising from a short rhizome which is anchored to the support plant by longish roots running under the fissures of the bark. The sheaths covering the internodes of the stems have expanded mouths and are covered with stiff hairs on the ridges. The leaves are ovate, apiculate, up to 3.5 cm long and 2.5 cm wide, convex on the adaxial surface (cockle-shaped) and hard-textured; the adaxial surface is olive, the abaxial green, stippled with purple.

The inflorescence is shorter than, and borne on the underside of, the leaf; it is about 1.7 cm long. The sepals are pale lemon-yellow, ovate, tapering at the apices, each having a linear nerve; the lateral sepals are connate for about one-third their length. The petals are wedge-shaped, unequally lobed with a broad waist at the base; they are yellow with a band of crimson bordering the inner margin. The lip is yellow and has two broad linear lobes.

	Length (cm)	Width (cm)
Median sepal	0.3	0.35
Lateral sepal	0.35	0.2
Petal	0.15	0.2
Lip	0.15	–
Flower	0.75	0.4

Flowering period   April to June.

Distribution   Endemic. Hollymount and Foxes' Gap.

Cultural notes   The same method may be employed as for *L. cochlearifolia* but the presence of leathery leaves would tend to suggest that drier conditions would be tolerable as long as the roots are kept moist.

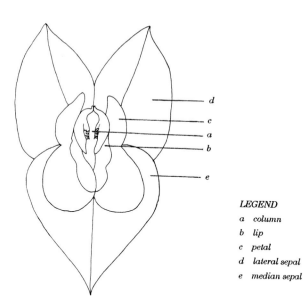

LEGEND

a   *column*
b   *lip*
c   *petal*
d   *lateral sepal*
e   *median sepal*

Lepanthes lanceolata

Description   *Lepanthes lanceolata* is an epiphytic species, plants of which consist of unifoliate stems up to 15 cm tall arising from a short rhizome which sprouts fine roots from the base. The nodes of the stems are covered with tubular sheaths, the mouths of which are apiculate and dilated. The leaves are elliptic-lanceolate, mucronate, up to 5 cm long and 2.1 cm wide, dark green on the adaxial surface and light green on the abaxial surface.

At maturity a bundle of racemes is borne in the axil of the leaf; the peduncles are up to 2.2 cm long. The sepals are red, each having a linear nerve; the lateral sepals are ovate and the median sepal subcordate. The petals are orange with an inner border of crimson and are bilobed, the anterior lobes being narrow and separated from the larger, peltate, posterior lobes by a cleft. The lip has two axe-shaped lobes closely appressed to the column, each having a claw at the centre; it is orange, tinged with red at the base.

	Length (cm)	Width (cm)
Median sepal	0.35	0.3
Lateral sepal	0.3	0.2
Petal	0.3	0.1
Lip	0.1	0.15
Column	0.1	–
Flower	0.6	0.45

Flowering period   August to October.

Distribution   Endemic. Fairy Glade and St James.

Cultural notes   Same as for *L. cochlearifolia*.

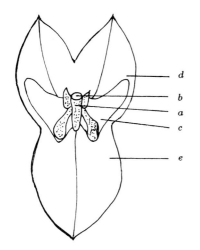

Lepanthes loddigesiana

Description *Lepanthes loddigesiana* is a miniature epiphytic plant bearing thin unifoliate stems radiating from a central rhizome which bears a cluster of fine roots. The stems are 1.5 - 5 cm tall and their internodes are covered by minutely hairy, ridged, tubular sheaths which have dilated apiculate mouths. The leaves are elliptical, mucronate, flat, thick-textured, pale green and 0.7 - 1 cm long and 0.6 - 0.8 cm wide.

The inflorescences are usually shorter than the leaves and one or more are borne in the leaf axils, each with only a few flowers. The sepals are pale yellow and ovate, the lateral sepals being two-thirds connate and acute. The median sepal is cucullate and apiculate. The petals are deltate, have a short basal claw, and a central band of violet on their posterior lobes flanking the violet column. The lip is violet with two arcuate lobes flanking a median apiculus which enfolds the column. The anther cap is white and there are two pollinia.

	Length (cm)	Width (cm)
Median sepal	0.15	0.2
Lateral sepal	0.15	0.07
Petal	0.05	0.07
Lip	0.02	0.02
Column	0.05	–
Flower	0.3	0.2

Flowering period   Year-round.

Distribution   Endemic. Uncommon Hill above Fruitul Vale, Corn Puss Gap, White Rock Hill, Hollymount, St Andrew, Portland and St Thomas.

Cultural notes   Same as for *L. cochlearifolia*.

Lepanthes multiflora

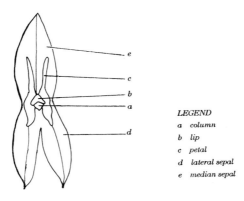

LEGEND
a   column
b   lip
c   petal
d   lateral sepal
e   median sepal

Description   *Lepanthes multiflora* is a lithophytic, terrestrial or epiphytic plant which has a tuft of unifoliate stems up to 2.3 cm long arising from a branched rhizome. The leaves are thick, shiny green, elliptic, up to 2 cm long and 0.5 cm wide.

The inflorescence is up to 4 cm long and bears tiny yellow flowers. The sepals are lanceolate, the median sepal being concave. The lateral sepals are connate for one-third of their length. The petals are clawed and have very narrow tapering anterior lobes and expanded posterior lobes. The lip has small rounded lateral lobes and is adnate to the column.

	Length (cm)	Width (cm)
Median sepal	0.3	0.15
Lateral sepal	0.3	0.1
Petal	0.05	0.15
Lip	0.1	0.2
Flower	0.7	0.3

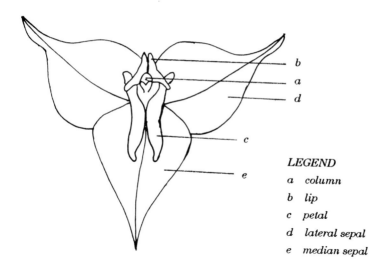

LEGEND

a   column
b   lip
c   petal
d   lateral sepal
e   median sepal

Lepanthes quadrata

Description *Lepanthes quadrata* is an epiphytic plant with several unifoliate stems rarely taller than 2 cm and clustered on a short rhizome. The stems are jointed, the internodes covered by sheaths having dilated apiculate mouths that are ciliolate on the ridges. The leaves are broadly elliptic, notched at the apices and light green with a suffusion of purple on the abaxial surfaces.

The inflorescences are branched and bundled together on the adaxial surfaces of the leaves. The flowers are wine-coloured with the sepals being ovate, apiculate and connate for one-third their length. The petals are linear, the posterior lobes narrower than the anterior ones; the lip is crimson, has a fleshy median lobe notched at the apex and two pointed lateral lobes that embrace the column which is green and is extended into a foot.

	Length (cm)	Width (cm)
Median sepal	0.25	0.2
Lateral sepal	0.3	0.2
Petal	0.3	0.1
Lip	0.15	0.15

Flowering period   Year-round.

Distribution   Endemic. Found in St Ann, Mt Diablo, the Blue and John Crow Mountains, Christiana and Douglas Castle District.

Cultural notes   Same as for *L. cochlearifolia*.

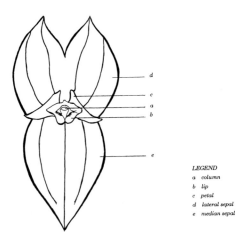

LEGEND
a   column
b   lip
c   petal
d   lateral sepal
e   median sepal

Lepanthes rotundata

Description   *Lepanthes rotundata* is a miniature epiphyte, about 2.5 cm tall on average, which grows in small tufts. The unifoliate stems are about 1.6 cm long, each bearing a single leaf and having the internodes covered by ridged sheaths with funnel-shaped mouths that have tapered apices; the ridges of the sheaths and the margins of the mouths have fine hairs. The leaves are oval or round, thick, almost flat, the midrib indistinct; they are up to 9 mm long and 6 - 8 mm wide. The peduncle is filiform, usually longer than the leaf, and held erectly away from it; it is about 1.2 - 1.5 cm long, sometimes bearing a maximum of two flowers simultaneously.

The flowers are small, pale yellow, transparent and usually resupinate. The median sepal is ovate, concave on the adaxial surface and has two lateral nerves flanking the median nerve. The lateral sepals are ovate, convex on the adaxial surface and connate for about two-thirds of their length; the tips are divaricate. Each of the latter has two nerves parallel to each other. The petals are deltate, tapering to a claw at the base, and placed diagonally at the base of the sepals. The lip has a small apiculus at the centre and is angular laterally where it encircles the column and ends in two peltate lobes below the column.

	Length (cm)	Width (cm)
Median sepal	0.35	0.25
Lateral sepal	0.35	0.15
Petal	0.2	0.15
Lip	0.1	0.2
Flower	0.7 - 0.9	0.3 - 0.4

Flowering period   June to February.

Distribution   Endemic. Arntully, Clydesdale and Foxes' Gap.

Cultural notes   Because of its small size, it is recommended that it be grown in a Wardian Case for those who grow orchids under lights, so as to keep the environment humid. The potting medium and growing conditions are the same as for *L. cochlearifolia*.

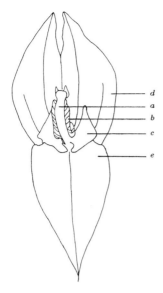

Lepanthes tridentata

Description   *Lepanthes tridentata* is one of the smaller species of the genus. The plant is epiphytic, has slender, clustered, erect, unifoliate, jointed stems up to 10 cm tall and is anchored to the supporting plant by fine roots. The internodes are covered by tubular sheaths which have very short setae on their ridges. The leaves are elliptic, tapered at their bases and notched at their apices, light green, up to 3.0 cm long and about 1.5 cm wide.

The inflorescences are racemes, two to five of which are borne in a bundle in the axil of the leaf lying flat on the adaxial surface of the latter. The peduncles are filiform, about 1.7 cm long, each bearing a few flowers which are minute and yellow with tinges of red.

The sepals are pale yellow and transparent, with the lateral sepals being ovate-lanceolate, concave at the base and connate for most of their length, each having a long linear nerve near the centre of the flower flanked by a shorter lateral nerve. The median sepal is ovate-lanceolate, apiculate, concave at the base, curves forward in the flower and has a median nerve. The petals are yellow, the posterior lobes each having a patch of vermilion; they are deltoid with a short claw, the anterior lobes being narrow. The lip is vermilion and has two linear divaricate lobes closely appressed to the column. The column is tinged with pink and is arched and deflexed.

	Length (cm)	Width (cm)
Median sepal	0.2 - 0.3	0.15
Lateral sepal	0.2 - 0.3	0.1
Petal	0.1	0.1 - 0.2
Lip	0.05 - 0.1	0.05
Flower	0.5 - 0.6	0.2 - 0.3
Column	0.1	0.05

Flowering period   January to October.

Distribution   Endemic. Fairy Glade, Portland, St Thomas and Blue Mountain Peak.

Cultural notes   Same as for *L. cochlearifolia*.

LEPANTHOPSIS

After *Lepanthes* and *opsis*,
resemblance; an allusion to
the similarity of this genus
to Lepanthes.

Lepanthopsis melanantha

Description *Lepanthopsis melanantha* is epiphytic and grows in thick clusters. Stems are 4.5 - 8 cm tall, have the internodes covered by tubular sheaths, the ridges and mouths of which are covered by setae; they arise from a short rhizome which bears fine purplish roots.

The leaves are thick, oval, narrowed to a short petiole and have a minute apiculus which is recurved; they are 2.8 - 3.5 cm long and 1.4 - 1.5 cm wide and are sometimes flecked with purple abaxially. Several inflorescences are borne in the axil of the leaf and are supported by the uppermost sheath, often twisting to the inflorescence which is about 2.6 cm long, bearing up to eight minute, dark crimson flowers in two ranks. The sepals are ovate and project forwards, the lateral sepals are paired and opposite the median sepal. The petals are triangular and much reduced, while the lip is scoop-shaped and rounded anteriorly.

	Length (cm)	Width (cm)
Median sepal	0.2	0.1
Lateral sepal	0.25	0.1
Petal	–	–
Lip	0.1	0.1
Column	0.05	–

Flowering period December to February.

Distribution Hollymount and Bellevue in Jamaica. Also found in Hispaniola and Cuba.

Cultural notes Plants can be grown in a wire basket in a mixture of sphagnum moss and charcoal, or on a piece of hardwood using coir fibre or sphagnum moss as a backing.

LIPARIS

From the Greek *liparos*, fatty, shiny; referring to the glossy surface of the leaves in many species.

Liparis elata

Description *Liparis elata* is terrestrial, characterized by conical pseudobulbs, each having about four nodes and bearing three to five plicate leaves. The pseudobulbs are about 4 cm tall and 2.5 cm wide at the base; concealed by pale green, overlapping scale leaves which are deciduous on older shoots. Soft, hairy, white roots sprout from the bases of the pseudobulbs. The leaves are broadly elliptic, soft-textured, pale green, up to 27.5 cm long and 6.6 cm wide and have long grooved petioles which overlap at their bases.

The inflorescence is a raceme arising from the apex of the pseudobulb; the peduncle is up to 38 cm long, purple and angular. The flowers are small, star-shaped and purple with a green column projecting from the centre. The sepals are linear, slightly recurved at the tips and point outwards. The petals are linear and jut downwards on either side of the ovary. The lip is heart-shaped with a narrow base, recurved and is tinged with green laterally. The column is pale green with the apex curved forwards. The ovary is pedicellate and has six low ridges along the grooves.

	Length (cm)	Width (cm)
Median sepal	0.6 - 0.8	0.1
Lateral sepal	0.6	0.1
Petal	0.7	0.05
Lip	0.5	0.35 - 0.5
Column	0.35	—

Flowering period   July to January.

Distribution   Hollymount, the Cockpit Country, St Elizabeth, St James, St Ann and St Andrew in Jamaica. Also found in Florida, Cuba, Mexico, Central America to Brazil, Ecuador, Peru and other Caribbean islands.

Cultural notes   A terrestrial mix is recommended. Keep well shaded.

Liparis saundersiana

Description   *Liparis saundersiana* is a terrestrial, unifoliate plant which has one or two corms growing closely together with roots sprouting from their bases. The corm is about 1.2 cm tall and 0.9 cm wide, compressed and covered by pale green scale leaves. A solitary pale green and cordate leaf enfolds the corms basally with its tubular petiole. The scape is up to 15 cm long, slender, hairy, reddish and bears a raceme at the apex.

The sepals are cream-coloured, lanceolate and translucent; the median sepal lying opposite to the lip in the same plane. The lateral sepals, together with the petals, underlie the surface of the lip. The petals are purple, linear filamentous, gradually tapering to a fine point. The lip is flat, roundly ovate, pale reddish-purple, translucent and enfolds the base of the column. The column is recurved over the surface of the lip.

	Length (cm)	Width (cm)
Median sepal	0.9	0.2
Lateral sepal	0.9	0.2
Petal	1.1	–
Lip	1.6	1.2
Column	0.3 - 0.4	–

Flowering period   October to December.

Distribution   Endemic. Hollymount, the Tobolski Mines and Chalk Hill.

Cultural notes   Grow the plant in a pot with a suitable terrestrial mix, adding some crushed leaf mould. Keep cool and moist.

LYCASTE

Lycaste is named for a Greek nymph, the daughter of Priam, last king of Troy.

Lycaste barringtoniae

Description   *Lycaste barringtoniae* may be lithophytic or epiphytic but is quite often found growing terrestrially. The plant has wrinkled pseudobulbs up to 9.5 cm tall and 6 cm wide, somewhat obliquely compressed and four-cornered, growing close together from a narrow rhizome with thick, hairy roots sprouting from the bases. Each pseudobulb bears two or three plaited dark green leaves which have strongly ribbed, narrow, overlapping petioles about 10 cm long. The leaves are ovate-lanceolate with tapering apices, up to 59 cm long and 14 cm wide.

The flowers are borne singly on scapes up to 7 cm long, arising from the bases of the pseudobulbs singly or in groups of two or three. They are heavy, fragrant, waxy, pendent, opening partially and are ochre or pale green with the apices of the perianth tipped with a darker olive green. The scape is covered by overlapping green helmet-shaped bracts, the flower being supported by a terminal bract which may be up to 2.7 cm long and sheaths the ovary of the flower.

The lateral sepals are falcate, fused beneath the column foot and overlapping ventrally to form a mentum with the latter, the apices pointing downwards. The petals are elliptic, apiculate, attached basally to the middle of the column, their apices spreading downwards.

The lip curves upwards in the flower being closely appressed against the curvature of the column, the anterior lobe forming a platform. The anterior lobe of the lip is pale yellow with fimbriate lateral margins, the apex being inrolled; it is separated by a wide isthmus from a narrow, triangular, cream, basal segment which has two apiculate lateral lobes and is thickened by fine carinae, the two outermost being very prominent. The carinae end in a ridge that borders a small depression at the base of the anterior lobe, coinciding with the apex of the column which is white, has a peaked anther cap and is extended into a column foot. There are two pollinia.

	Length (cm)	Width (cm)
Median sepal	4.0 - 4.6	1.5 - 1.7
Lateral sepal	4.0 - 4.5	1.7 - 1.9
Petal	4.0 - 4.2	1.3 - 1.4
Lip	3.5 - 4.2	1.7 - 1.9
Column	2.8 - 3.0	0.5

Flowering period   April to July.

Distribution   Arntully, the Cockpit Country, Hollymount and the Red Light District in Jamaica. Also found in Cuba and Hispaniola.

Cultural notes   This plant is best grown in a basket with large pieces of charcoal and leaf mould as a medium. Keep well shaded and well drained, as the pseudobulbs are very susceptible to decay.

MACRADENIA

From the Greek *makros*, long and *aden*, gland; referring to the long, linear-spathulate stipe connecting the pollinia to the gland or viscid disk.

Macradenia lutescens

Description *Macradenia lutescens* is epiphytic with narrow, cylindrical unifoliate pseudobulbs up to 4.7 cm long and 0.5 cm wide. The pseudobulbs are dark green, lightly ribbed, covered by scarious scale leaves and are grouped closely together on a short rhizome bearing fine whitish roots. The leaves are leathery, dark glossy green, linear-elliptic, up to 14 cm long and up to 3 cm wide; the midrib is prominent.

The flowers are small, pendulous and are borne in a loose panicle up to 11 cm long emerging from the base of the pseudobulb. The sepals are elliptic, olive green with a tinge of reddish-brown, the keeled median sepal projecting outwards. The petals are lanceolate, olive green with a central linear reddish-brown blotch. The lip is non-resupinate, triangular, waxy, with the apex drawn out into a fine filament and curling backwards. The mid-line of the lip is marked by three linear pale pink calli and one or sometimes two pink veins on either side. The side lobes of the lip curve upwards. The column is erect.

	Length (cm)	Width (cm)
Median sepal	1.3	0.5
Lateral sepal	1.0	0.3
Petal	1.1	0.3
Lip	0.45	0.6
Column	0.7	0.3

Flowering period   October to May.

Distribution   The Cockpit Country, Golden Spring, Hollymount and Lydford in Jamaica. Also found in Florida, from Colombia to the Guianas, Cuba and Trinidad.

Cultural notes The plant adapts easily to slab or pot culture. Keep well shaded.

MALAXIS

From the Greek *malaxis*, softening; after the soft and tender foliar texture.

Malaxis spicata

Description *Malaxis spicata* is a terrestrial plant which grows in leaf mould. When mature it has two leaves overlapping each other at the base of the petioles and enclosing a pale green, wedge-shaped pseudobulb. The petioles are 7 - 8 cm long; the leaf blades are soft textured, ovate, acuminate, glossy green, keeled at the base and up to 12 cm long and 6 cm wide.

The inflorescence is a spike arising from the axil of the upper leaf; the peduncle is four-angled and up to 23 cm long. The pedicels are about 0.6 cm long. The flowers are non-resupinate (lip uppermost) and green. The petals and sepals are deflexed, the median sepal only slightly. The lip has two posterior lobes protruding beyond the column and a sharply pointed anterior lobe; it is concave on the disc and has a thin green line encircling the base of the column and extending in a band towards the apex.

	Length (cm)	Width (cm)
Median sepal	0.35	0.15
Lateral sepal	0.25	0.1
Petal	0.25	0.1
Lip	0.35	0.25

Flowering period   September to January.

Distribution   The Cockpit Country, John Crow Mountains, St Ann, Hardwar Gap, St Catherine's Peak and Hollymount in Jamaica. Also found in Florida, the Greater Antilles, Martinique and Dominica.

Cultural notes   The same type of culture as for other shade-loving terrestrials. Our mixture comprises coarse sand, leaf mould, bagasse and tree-fern siftings in equal proportions.

MAXILLARIA

From the Latin *maxilla*, jaw,
jawbone; the flowers of some
species supposedly resemble
the jaws of an insect.

Maxillaria alba

Description *Maxillaria alba* is an epiphyte consisting of a
cluster of narrow trailing stems, up to 45 cm long, sometimes
branching, growing from a short, common, basal rhizome bearing a set of fine roots which anchor the plant to its support. The
pseudobulbs are flat, compressed, slightly wrinkled, curved,
expanded towards the apex and narrow at the base, about
4.6 cm long and 2 cm wide at their widest point. They are
arranged in two ranks crowded along the stem and are covered
at the base by several pairs of imbricating scale leaves which
also cover the interconnecting sections of the rhizome. The
scale leaves also conceal those roots which run linearly along
the stem; at maturity they are hardened and tan- coloured with
only the basal halves remaining. The leaves are linear-lanceo-

late, folded along the midrib at the base and are 27.5 cm long and 1.8 cm wide.

The flowers are cream-coloured and are borne singly on pedicels about 4 cm long in the axils of sheaths which overlap the immature pseudobulbs found at the tips of the stems. The sepals are linear-lanceolate and point towards the corners of a triangle, with the median sepals shielding the column and overlapping the petals. The petals are linear-lanceolate, narrower than the sepals and are attached obliquely to the base of the column. The lip is tinged with yellow, is scoop-shaped with erect lateral lobes and has a smooth central callus about 4 mm long and 2.3 mm wide; it articulates at the base with the column foot. The column is extended into a short foot at the base and curves forward in the flower.

	Length (cm)	Width (cm)
Median sepal	1.6	0.6
Lateral sepal	1.9	0.3
Petal	1.3	0.5
Lip	1.3	0.8
Column	1.0	0.25

Flowering period   July to March.

Distribution   Arntully, the Cockpit Country and Hollymount in Jamaica. Also found in Guatemala, Venezuela, Brazil, Cuba and Trinidad.

Cultural notes   Mounting the plant on a tree-fern slab enhances growth. The plant may also be placed in a basket with charcoal and tree-fern fibre as the medium.

Maxillaria crassifolia

Description   *Maxillaria crassifolia* is lithophytic or epi-phytic. The plant consists of leafy shoots arising parallel to each other in tight tufts from a horizontal rhizome. The leaves are thick, leathery, linear, tapering at the apices; up to 38 cm long and longer and 2.5 cm wide, dark green, folded along the midrib, overlapping at their bases and spreading outwards as a group to form a fan. Each tuft has two or three short overlapping scale leaves at the base which become dark brown as they mature. The innermost leaf is fused and swollen at the base and attached to a very short pseudobulb.

The solitary inflorescence is axillary and bears a single flower; the peduncle is about 2.2 cm long and the pedicellate ovary 2 cm long. The flowers are waxy, yellow, have floral segments overlapping to form a tube and appear to be self-pollinated. The sepals are ovate, apiculate and keeled; the petals are ligulate and the lip is scoop-shaped with the lateral lobes upturned. The lip has a flattened crest about 1 cm long on the disc; the column is erect.

	Length (cm)	Width (cm)
Median sepal	1.3	0.45
Lateral sepal	1.6	0.5
Petal	1.2	0.25
Lip	1.4	0.6
Column	0.8-1.0	0.3

Flowering period   October to March.

Distribution   Arntully, the Cockpit Country, Hardwar Gap and Hollymount in Jamaica. Also found in Cuba, Hispaniola, Florida, Mexico, Central America, Venezuela and Brazil.

Cultural notes   This plant adapts well to potting in tree fern, to basket culture and to slabbing on tree fern or pieces of hard wood. Keep in medium shade.

Maxillaria purpurea

Description   *Maxillaria purpurea* is epiphytic with a long narrow rhizome bearing flattened pseudobulbs at regular intervals which are more widely spaced in older than younger plants. Long, straight, fine roots run from the overlapping scale leaves. The leaves are bright green, linear-lanceolate, up to 22 cm long and 1.5 - 2 cm wide.

The flowers are pale yellow, each being borne on a pedicel up to 1.2 cm long arising from the axils of the scale leaves in groups of about eight. The sepals are ovate-apiculate, concave and overlap the petals and lip. The petals are narrower than the sepals. The lip is scoop-shaped, apiculate, with upright, rounded, lateral lobes and a triangular front lobe which is bright gold at the tip. It is crystalline and has a transverse ridge between the front lobes and the lateral lobes. There are three linear nerves and two round glands at the base of the lip.

	Length (cm)	Width (cm)
Median sepal	0.7	0.35
Lateral sepal	0.5	0.35
Petal	0.4	0.25
Lip	0.35	0.4
Column	0.3	0.1

Flowering period   August to April.

Distribution   Between Newcastle and Hardwar Gap, Mount Airy, Trelawny, St Ann and the John Crow Mountains in Jamaica. Also found in Cuba, Hispaniola and from Brazil to Peru.

Cultural notes   This species makes an interesting basket plant although it has been grown successfully on tree-fern slabs and poles. Keep in medium shade.

Maxillaria rufescens var. minor

Description   *Maxillaria rufescens* var. *minor* is an epiphyte with small pseudobulbs arising from a horizontal rhizome. The pseudobulbs are dull green, ellipsoidal, four-angled, slightly ribbed, about 2 cm long and 1.4 cm wide. The leaves are borne singly at the apex of the pseudobulb; they are linear-lanceolate, up to 10.5 cm long and 1.9 cm wide.

The flowers are solitary, have pedicellate ovaries about 1 cm long and are borne on peduncles which are about 2.2 cm long; they are translucent, pale yellow and have a span of about 2 cm. The median sepal is ovate and concave; the lateral sepal is obovate with linear nerves and rounded apices. The petals are linear-ovate, each with a basal cleft on the anterior margin; they are paired about the column and partly covered by the overlapping median sepal. The lip is yellow with purple spots and trilobed; the lateral lobes with pointed apices emerging near the base. There is a linear callus on the midline of the lip.

	Length (cm)	Width (cm)
Median sepal	1.2	0.7
Lateral sepal	1.2	0.7
Petal	1.2	0.5
Lip	0.9	0.6
Column	0.7	–

Flowering period   April to September.

Distribution   Hollymount and the St Andrew hills in Jamaica. Also found in Cuba and elsewhere in tropical America.

Cultural notes   Plant thrives on tree-fern slabs or in pots in a medium of tree fern and charcoal. Keep well shaded.

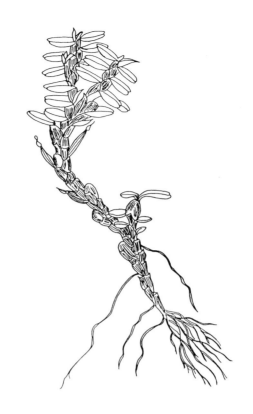

Maxillaria swartziana

Description *Maxillaria swartziana* is a lithophytic or epi-phytic plant which has a creeping, branching, flattened, jointed stem arising from a horizontal rhizome. The internodes of the stem are completely covered by the overlapping sheathing bases of the leaves.

The pseudobulbs are borne at varying intervals along the stem and very often at the apices of the branches in the axils of the leaves. The leaves are linear, dark green, notched at the apices and have their laminae spread flat; they are up to 4 cm long and 1 cm wide.

The flowers are purple and in very rare cases yellow. The sepals and petals are ovate. The lateral sepals are joined together to form a chin at the base. The column is cylindrical and curved. The lip is scoop-shaped and clawed at the base.

	Length (cm)	Width (cm)
Median sepal	0.3	0.15
Lateral sepal	0.3	0.15
Petal	0.7	0.4
Lip	0.6	0.25
Column	0.5	–

Flowering period   November to February.

Distribution   Endemic. Bellevue and the Red Light District.

Cultural notes   The plant grows well in a basket with pea-grain-sized charcoal or gravel and shredded tree fern. Keep well shaded.

NEOCOGNIAUXIA

From the Greek *neos*, new; a second generic name after Alfred Cogniaux, an eminent nineteenth/twentieth-century Belgian botanist who wrote extensively on the orchids of Brazil and the West Indies.

Neocogniauxia monophylla

Description *Neocogniauxia monophylla* is a small epiphytic plant with a cluster of upright unifoliate stems arising from a short rhizome which sprouts thickish white roots. The stems are about 7 cm tall and 0.5 cm thick, very slender, covered with hardened brown-speckled sheathing scale leaves; each stem bears a solitary, terminal, elliptical, leathery, rigid, dark green leaf. The leaves may be up to 7.8 cm long and 1.1 cm wide.

The solitary inflorescence arises from the leaf axil and is 15 - 20 cm long, usually bearing one flower (rarely two), the peduncle having light green bands alternating with dark brown sheathing bracts. The perianth is bright orange as is the column. The sepals and petals are spread out flat; the sepals are ovate, the petals are obovate, overlapping slightly at the base of the column. The column is perpendicular to the axis of the flower and is partially enfolded by the two lateral lobes of the lip. The anterior lobe of the lip has a slightly crenate margin and the disc has short reddish papillae.

	Length (cm)	Width (cm)
Median sepal	2.3	1.1
Lateral sepal	2.3	1.1
Petal	2.1	1.1
Lip	0.9	0.8
Column	0.9	–

Flowering period August to September.

Distribution Endemic. Fairy Glade, Foxes' Gap and Johnson Mountain.

Cultural notes The plant prospers when grown either in sphagnum moss alone or in a pot of shredded tree fern with a top dressing of sphagnum. The plants should be kept moist with good air movement since their natural habitat is the cloud forest at over 1200 m (4000 ft). Keep well shaded.

OCTADESMIA

From the Greek *okta*, eightfold and
desmos, bond; from the eight pollen
masses.

Octadesmia (Dilomilis) montana

Description   *Octadesmia (Dilomilis) montana* is epiphytic
and grows in tufts up to 90 cm high with shoots bearing leaves
towards the upper portions of older stems. The bases of the
stems are slightly swollen where they emerge from the rhizome
and have thick roots. The leaves are thin-textured, linear-
lanceolate, decurrent, distichous, up to 9.5 cm long and longer
and 1 cm wide.

The inflorescence is a raceme more than 10 cm long with
several iridescent white flowers all opening simultaneously,
but with the lower ones being larger than those near the tip.
The median sepal is linear-lanceolate and is flanked by two
crescent-shaped petals curving outwards; the lateral sepals are
shorter than the median sepal and point downwards behind
the lip.

The lip is trilobed with both lateral pointed lobes curving
slightly towards the column, the front lobe projecting slightly

forwards and curling under at the margin. The lip has two linear crests and has short reddish veins in the centre running towards the base.

	Length (cm)	Width (cm)
Median sepal	1.6	0.45
Lateral sepal	1.4	0.4
Petal	1.6	0.3
Lip	0.7	1.4
Column	0.65	–

Flowering period   November to March.

Distribution   Fairy Glade, Foxes' Gap and the hills behind Hardwar Gap in Jamaica. Also found in Santo Domingo, Cuba and Puerto Rico.

Cultural notes   In Jamaica this plant grows in the cloud forest area. The plants therefore should be kept cool and moist with a temperature range of 7 - 21° C (45 - 70° F). The plants do well in a shallow basket or in a pot with equal parts of sphagnum moss and leaf mould, or in gravel alone. They should be kept well shaded.

OECEOCLADES

From the Greek *oikeios*, private and *klados*, branch; referring to Lindley's separation of certain species from *Angraecum* to form a distinct tribe or "private branch".

Oeceoclades maculata (Eulophidium maculatum)

Description   *Oeceoclades maculata* is terrestrial with cuneate (wedge-shaped) pseudobulbs, 2.7 cm tall, each bearing a solitary, stiff, spathulate leaf, tapered and folded along the midrib at the base. The leaves are marbled dark and pale green and are up to 18 cm long and 5 cm wide.

The inflorescence is a raceme, the peduncles arising singly from the bases of the pseudobulbs and bearing scale leaves at the nodes. The number of flowers may be up to fourteen per inflorescence. The lateral sepals are elliptic and olive; the median sepal is linear-lanceolate, concave, olive and inclining towards the lip. The petals are linear-lanceolate, dull cream, translucent, overlapping at the bases and closely appressed to the median sepal.

. The four-lobed lip is flanked on either side by the lateral sepals; is white, fiddle-shaped with a wide isthmus separating the upper lobes from the lower ones. There are two small, upright, white, triangular crests at the base of the lip marking the aperture leading to the small saccate basal spur; the upper lobes have fine, dark rose-coloured veins and curve towards the column. The lip is dorsally keeled, apiculate, and has two linear rose blotches on either side of the isthmus which spread into the lower lobes. The column is white with faint rose stripes on the under surface and curves forward over the disc of the lip.

	Length (cm)	Width (cm)
Median sepal	1.2	0.3
Lateral sepal	1.2	0.2
Petal	1.2	0.3
Lip	0.9	1.0
Spur	0.5	–
Column	0.4-0.5	–

Flowering period   August to October.

Distribution   Fairly widespread on wooded hillsides in Jamaica. Also found in Brazil, Paraguay, French Guiana, Venezuela, South Florida and tropical Africa from Senegal to Angola and Zimbabwe, Tanzania, Zanzibar and Pemba.

Cultural notes   Plants may be grown as described for other terrestrials. Keep well shaded.

NB This plant putatively arrived from Africa during the early 1950s when a red haze from the Sahara entered the western hemisphere. The plant appeared first in Brazil from where it spread throughout the Caribbean islands and into the southern states of the USA via Central America.

ONCIDIUM

From the Greek diminutive of *onkos*, tumor or swelling; after the warty calluses on the lip of all species in the genus.

Oncidium gauntlettii

Description   *Oncidium gauntlettii* is an epiphytic plant which has thickened, stiff leaves arranged in a fan like those of the other equitant oncidiums to which it is related. The leaves are about 4 cm long and 5 mm wide and are strongly keeled, the adaxial (upper) surfaces being only a shallow groove. The roots are fine and glabrous. Several plantlets (fans) are sometimes clustered on a common rhizome.

The inflorescence arises from the axil of one of the lower leaves and seldom bears more than two flowers on a peduncle about 8.5 cm long. The lateral sepals are linear, cream-coloured, streaked with brown, connate with the tips free and curling backwards. The median sepal is rose, linear-lanceolate; the petals are pale rose and lanceolate.

The lip is the most prominent part of the flower; it is flat, trilobed, the two upper lobes being very pale lilac, finely serrated at the margins and slanting inwards towards the centre of the lip. The front lobe is lilac, the margin rounded, undulated, with a slightly keeled median cleft. The disc of the lip is a pale yellow with a minute, cream-coloured mound at the centre of the base surrounded by a thin red line. The column is pale green and globular with two minute apiculate wings.

	Length (cm)	Width (cm)
Median sepal	0.7	0.15
Lateral sepal	0.6	0.3
Petal	0.8	0.2
Lip	1.1	1.2
Column	0.2	–

Flowering period September to April.

Distribution   Endemic. Dolphin Head, Hollymount, Woodstock and Chalky Hill.

Cultural notes The plant thrives on slabs of tree fern root or hard wood, or in thumb pots with small pieces of charcoal or gravel as medium. Keep in medium shade.

Hybridization One hybrid has been recorded with *Oncidium triquetrum* to produce *O. Rose de Mask*.

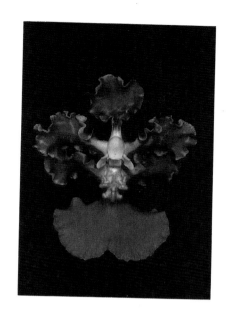

Oncidium luridum (altissimum)

Description *Oncidium luridum* is a rather heavy epiphytic plant found in various ecological niches, on rocks, trees or in soil. The leaves are large, leathery, ovate-lanceolate, strongly keeled, up to 60 cm long and longer, 12 cm wide and sometimes wider. They are bright, glossy green when young or protected by heavy shade, but when mature or exposed to sunlight they develop dark reddish-purple spots. The leaves are produced singly from a small pseudobulb 1 - 2 cm long and 1.5 - 2.5 cm in diameter. The pseudobulbs are completely concealed by overlapping scale leaves and are interconnected by a short rhizome.

The inflorescence is a loose panicle with secondary and tertiary branches and sometimes attains a length of 3 m. The flowers are borne singly or in groups of twos or threes on the ultimate branches; they have a span of about 4.3 cm, are mustard-coloured, sometimes tinged with green, and have a pattern of confluent brown dots which are paler on the lip than on other perianth parts. In some instances the concentration of brown dots is so heavy that hardly any of the background colour shows through. In rare specimens the background is bright golden yellow and then only a few spots are present. A pure yellow form is also known. Some clones from Guyana and Trinidad have greenish flowers.

The petals and sepals are obovate, clawed with undulate margins and have a crisp texture; the dorsal sepal is spathulate and has a long claw. The lateral sepals and petals are paired, each pair spreading horizontally above the lip and inclining backwards. Basally the lip has two lateral, oblong, dark brown lobes with their margins inrolled dorsally, separated by a short claw which expands into the crest which is about 8 mm wide. The anterior lobe of the lip is reniform with a central cleft. The crest has two upper tubercles and lower ones divided by a central ridge, the papillae on the outer tubercles being rose-coloured and the central ridges are bright golden yellow at the base. Two thin dark bands of reddish-brown extend halfway up the sides of the crest from the front lobe of the lip. The column is ivory and has a peaked anther cap and column wings which are sometimes tinged with rose-lavender and are lobed and waxy. The two waxy pollinia are bright orange.

	Length (cm)	Width (cm)
Median sepal	1.8 - 1.9	0.9 - 1.1
Lateral sepal	1.6 - 1.7	0.6 - 0.7
Petal	1.6 - 2.0	0.8 - 1.1
Lip	1.6 - 1.9	1.8 - 2.0
Column	0.5	0.5

Flowering period April to October.

Distribution Widespread throughout the island. Also found in Florida, Trinidad, the Lesser Antilles, Mexico, Central America, Colombia, Venezuela, Guyana, Brazil and Peru.

Cultural notes This species is susceptible to crown rot and should therefore be kept from damp, moist locations. Areas with good air movement are suitable. It adapts well to almost any type of culture.

Hybridization This species has been hybridized with other oncidiums.

Oncidium pulchellum

Description   *Oncidium pulchellum* is epiphytic and has shoots growing closely together from a very short rhizome with fine, white, glabrous roots emerging from their bases. Overlapping, dry, papery, scale leaves are found at the base of each shoot. The leaves are arranged in two rows, overlapping closely at the base and spreading outwards to form a fan (hence the descriptive name, equitant, for the leaves which overlap in two ranks). The leaves are thick, conduplicate and keeled, shiny green, sometimes brownish along the margins and suffused with purple; the midrib is strongly curved. The leaves are up to 18 cm long and are 1.9 - 2 cm wide. There is a much reduced, flattened pseudobulb, about 1.3 cm long, found in the axil of the uppermost leaves.

The inflorescence is an axillary raceme, the scape of varying lengths, but in robust specimens may be as long as 100 cm. The flowers show a wide variation in colour, some alba forms occurring, but others vary from pale lavender, pink and mauve to deep lavender-pink; some flowers may have one hue but others may be variously patterned with darker veins, or darker flowers may have a white margin.

The petals are spathulate, sometimes having a few spots or bars at the base; the lateral sepals are joined for about two-thirds of their length, the apices curling backwards. The median sepal is clawed, apiculate with undulate margins. The petals are spread out on either side of the column; they are spathulate, clawed and have undulate margins but are wider than the sepals; there is a brown band at the base of the claw and sometimes minute brown spots.

The lip is four-lobed, the margins undulate; the lower anterior lobes are separated by a deep cleft and are incurved at the margins, making the lip slightly concave. The upper lobes are shorter and narrower than the lower ones and these may be fully rounded or toothed on the lower margin, but touching or overlapping the lower lobes. There is a triangular crest at the base of the lip which is spotted with dark orange, the background colour being white; the callus may be white or yellow with six to nine papillae. The column has a beaked anther cap and column wings which may be white, rose or dark lavender; the stigmatic surface is fully exposed.

	Length (cm)	Width (cm)
Median sepal	0.9	0.45
Synsepalum	1.2	0.45
Petal	1.1	0.75
Lip	2.1 - 3.0	2.5 - 3.3
Column	0.3 - 0.4	–

Flowering period   May to June.

Distribution   Endemic. Found in Brown's Town and nearby areas, Manchester, the Cockpit Country and the Mandeville hills.

Cultural notes   The plant flourishes on twigs and slabs but may be potted in a thumb pot in a medium of tree fern or fine pieces of charcoal or gravel. Water that is hard tends to leave calcareous deposits on the plants, so rain water is ideal. The plant is susceptible to Boisduval scale.

Hybridization   This plant has been widely hybridized with other equitant oncidiums and their hybrids.

NB   Plants exposed to intense sunlight tend to have intense reddish-purple flowers and leaves. Keep in light to medium shade.

Oncidium tetrapetalum

Description   *Oncidium tetrapetalum* is epiphytic and has small shoots clustered close together on a short rhizome, each shoot consisting of a fan of equitant leaves protected at the base by papery, overlapping, sheathing scale leaves. White, glabrous roots arise from the base of each shoot. The leaves are thick, triquetrous, light green, or suffused with purple pigment, about 20 cm at maximum length and 1 cm wide.

The inflorescence is a branched raceme, the scape varying between 20 to 70 cm in length. The flowers are resupinate, sometimes fragrant and borne on pedicels about 1.3 cm long. The median sepal is concave on the adaxial surface and heavily barred with brown. The lateral sepals are connate for most of their length, the apices remaining free and curling backwards. This synsepalum is held horizontally, away from the lip. The petals are lobed, slightly fluted and usually barred with confluent brown specks, the apices having the same colour as the lip.

The lip is four-lobed, the upper lobes being small, narrow,[1] slightly reflexed and flanking a shield-shaped crest, which is separated from the anterior segment of the lip by a narrow isthmus[2]. The anterior segment is bilobed and either kidney-shaped with a wide median cleft or having a narrow incision between the lobes; the margins are rounded and crenulate.

The colour of the lip is always the same as the background colour of the petals and this may be white, white tinged with rose or lavender flushed with rose, or any combination of these. (In the alba form, the petals and sepals are pure white like the lip.) The crest is heavily barred with reddish-brown and the callus has eight yellow protuberances, two lateral ones flanking two sets of three arranged one above the other. The column is white or greenish with a beaked anther cap and two column wings which may be white or tinged with rose.

NB There are two varieties of *O. tetrapetalum* which show a difference in the form of the lip. In Type 1 the anterior segment of the lip is reniform, but in Type 2 the flower is larger and the anterior lobes are separated by a narrow incision, so the lip has a "full-skirted" appearance. Measurements are given for both types. A range of types exists between these two extremes which should not to be confused with the hybrid swarm of the *O. tetrapetalum* x *O. pulchellum* complex.

Type 1

	Length (cm)	Width (cm)
Median sepal	0.7	0.2
Synsepalum	0.7	0.35
Petal	0.7	0.45 - 0.5
Lip	0.7 - 1.1	0.5 - 1.3
Column	0.4	–

Type 2

	Length (cm)	Width (cm)
Median sepal	0.8	0.25
Synsepalum	0.7	0.4
Petal	0.8	0.45
Lip	1.6	1.6
Column	0.4	–

[1] In *O. pulchellum* these lobes are much larger and touch or overlap the anterior lobes.
[2] The presence of a dot behind the isthmus is used as a diagnostic feature to distinguish *O. tetrapetalum* from *O. pulchellum*.

Flowering period Year-round.

Distribution Endemic. Knockpatrick, May Pen, Moneague, South West Point and Spring Garden, Trelawny.

Cultural notes Slab or pot culture may be used for these plants. Keep well illuminated.

Hybridization This species has been little used in hybridization.

Oncidium triquetrum

Description *Oncidium triquetrum* is an equitant epiphyte. The leaves are normally dark or medium green but may develop reddish-brown pigments when exposed to a fair amount of light. They are 15 - 20 cm long in larger specimens and 1 - 1.2 cm wide on average, are linear with tapering apices, strongly keeled dorsally, the upper surfaces remaining almost flat so that they are three-cornered and overlap basally in two rows to form a fan, concealing a small leafless pseudobulb.

The peduncle is axillary, up to 27 cm long and longer, jointed with short papery bracts at the nodes and bears a cluster of five to fourteen flowers on pedicels 1.4 - 1.6 cm long. The flowers are small, the span rarely exceeding 2.3 cm; firm, slightly waxy and last about one week. The sepals are slightly concave, have a background colour of cream and are blotched with reddish-brown pigment on their inner surfaces. The median sepal is ovate-lanceolate with a very pointed apex and inclines upwards above the column. The lateral sepals are joined to form a synsepalum and have a bifid apex.

The petals are slightly clawed, ovate-lanceolate, with slightly crenulate margins, cream with a streak of reddish-brown along the median line and spread out horizontally above the lip giving a winged appearance to the flower. The lip is shield-shaped with two rounded lateral lobes separated from the deltoid anterior lobe by two lateral clefts; the margin is crenulate and the central portion of the lip is patterned with a suffusion of tan or reddish-brown pigments.

A small yellow mound of tissue forms the crest at the centre of the lip. The column is 4 mm long, perpendicular to the lip and pale yellow like the wings which it bears; the column wings are up to 2.5 mm long and are apiculate.

	Length (cm)	Width (cm)
Median sepal	1.0 - 1.3	0.45 - 0.6
Synsepalum	0.8 - 1.0	0.5 - 0.6
Petal	1.0 - 1.3	0.5 - 0.7
Lip	1.1 - 1.4	1.0 - 1.3
Column	0.4	–

Flowering period Year-round with a peak period from June to October.

Distribution Endemic. The Cockpit Country, St James, Hollymount, Portland, St Thomas, Worthy Park and rarely in St Andrew.

Cultural notes This plant adapts well to potting in small containers or to slab culture on tree-fern or cork, or pieces of hardwood. Longevity exceeding five years is doubtful. Keep well shaded.

Hybridization *Oncidium triquetrum* has been hybridized with other equitant *Oncidium* species. Hybrids achieve new and interesting patterns due to the mask on the lip. *Oncidium triquetrum* genes are present in more than 55 per cent of all registered equitant *Oncidium* hybrids. It is also compatible with *Rodriguezia* and has been hybridized with at least one species in this genus to produce a *Rodricidium*.

NB A pure yellow form is known.

PELEXIA

From the Greek *pelex*, helmet;
probably referring to the dorsal
sepal which is united with the
petals to form a narrow helmet.

Pelexia setacea

Description Plants of *Pelexia setacea* are terrestrial, growing
in tufts, each consisting of a solitary leaf held erect on its long
petiole with a cluster of fleshy, hairy, cream-coloured roots
sprouting from the base. The leaf blade is glossy, bright green,
up to about 16.5 cm long and 5.1 cm wide with a prominent
midrib protruding on the under surface and extending into the
petiole. The petiole is reddish-tan and up to 17 cm long in larger
specimens. The scapes may be as tall as 65 cm and together
with the petiole are covered with papery brown bracts at the
base.

The flowers number about ten per inflorescence and are
spirally arranged at the top of the scape; they have twisted
pedicellate ovaries about 2 cm long. The median sepal is pale
green, lanceolate, acuminate, concave at the base where it
forms a pouch, the margins overlapping the base of the lip
forming a tube. The lateral sepals are greenish-cream, linear-
lanceolate, acuminate, overlapping the lip basally to form a
spur.

The lip is pale green with a white, pointed fimbriate front lobe and base extending into a narrow trough of the median sepal. The petals are cream, arcuate and closely appressed to the median sepal, their outer margins forming a border. The column is white and has linear pollinia.

	Length (cm)	Width (cm)
Median sepal	2.9 - 3.3	0.6
Lateral sepal	4.1	0.3
Petal	1.6 - 2.0	0.25
Lip	1.2 - 1.9	0.6

Flowering period   December to February.

Distribution   Hollymount, Clarendon, St Elizabeth, Trelawny and the Red Light District in Jamaica. Also in northern South America, the Bahamas and the Greater Antilles.

Cultural notes   Potting in a mixture of leaf mould and tree fern is recommended. Keep well shaded.

PHAIUS

From the Greek *phaios*, grey or swarthy, the predominantly brownish hue of the flowers.

Phaius tankervilleae

(Nun Orchid)

Description *Phaius tankervilleae* is a terrestrial with short, conical pseudobulbs 8.5 cm long which have several longitudinal ridges and are interconnected by a rhizomatous stem. The pseudobulbs are covered by overlapping plicate leaves when young, but older pseudobulbs may bear only two to three leaves at the apex. The leaves are ovate-lanceolate, thin-textured and dark glossy green; each can be as long as 93 cm in mature specimens and 13.6 cm wide. The leaves have prominent veins, the midrib being the strongest. The pseudobulbs have many nodes; the older ones retain the veins of decayed leaves which present a spiny appearance. Thick hairy roots sprout from the bases of the pseudobulbs.

The terminal inflorescence is an erect raceme with a stout peduncle up to 103 cm long sheathed at the nodes by pale green bracts. About twelve flowers are borne on each inflorescence on pale greenish-white pedicels 3.6 - 4.8 cm long; the flowers are pendent with the petals and sepals spreading outwards like a fan above the lip which hangs downwards. The median sepal and the petals are linear-lanceolate; the lateral sepals arcuate, all of them being cream on their lower surface and pale tan on the upper (adaxial) surfaces. The dorsal sepal shields the column by inclining towards it.

The lip is roughly triangular when spread out, is divided into three lobes anteriorly and has a small basal spur; the margin is slightly crenulate and rolled under. The median lobe is pale rose changing to light apricot in older flowers; the side lobes are dark maroon, streaked with cream-coloured nerves. The median crest at the entrance to the tube formed by the lip, is flanked by two lateral pale yellow crests which extend half-way up the tube. The column is ivory-coloured, 1.8 cm long and protected by the overlapping base of the lip which forms a tube around it.

	Length (cm)	Width (cm)
Median sepal	4.0 - 5.0	1.2
Lateral sepal	3.9 - 5.0	1.1 - 1.3
Petal	3.6 - 4.7	0.9 - 1.0
Lip	3.6 - 4.2	3.0 - 3.7
Column	1.9	—

Flowering period   April to June.

Distribution   Hollymount, Hope River Valley, the Red Light District and St Ann in Jamaica. Also introduced and naturalized in Cuba, Panama and Hawaii. Native to northern India, Malaysia, Indonesia, Australia and some Pacific islands.

Cultural notes   As for other terrestrials; medium shade.

NB Dulcie Powell[1] notes that the plant was imported from China in 1787 by Hinton East Esq. as *Limodorum Tankervilleae*. It was planted in East's garden near what is today Gordon Town, St Andrew but which was then part of a property called Spring Garden. The lowland area to which it belonged was commonly called Liguanea. It was from East's garden that the plants have spread.

[1]D. Powell. 1972. "The Botanic Garden, Liguanea (with a revision of Hortus Eastensis)." *Bulletin of the Institute of Jamaica* (Science Series) 15, Part 1: 1-94.

PLEUROTHALLIS

From the Greek *pleuron*, rib and *thallos*, branch; a reference to the many leaf-bearing, rib-like stems arising caespitosely in many species.

Pleurothallis corniculata

Description   *Pleurothallis corniculata* is epiphytic with a short rhizome bearing very short stems up to 3.5 mm long and having a cluster of tangled roots adhering to the supporting plant. The leaves are thick, leathery, keeled, ovate-elliptic; 12.9 cm long and 3.5 - 8 mm wide.

Two or three inflorescences are borne in the axil of each leaf. The peduncles are thread-like and 1.5 - 3.7 cm long, each having a solitary flower often cleistogamous. The sepals are ovate-lanceolate, crystalline and ochre with a dark red median nerve flanked by two lateral nerves. The lateral sepals are paired and connate to the apex and expanded at the base to form a chin. The petals are triangular with a broad fimbriate apex and taper to a narrow base.

The lip is ochre, trough-shaped with a narrow basal isthmus and a ligulate limb; it has two prominent linear calli flanking a short median callus on the anterior lobe. The lateral lobes of the lip are oblong, fimbriate and are suffused with a dark reddish-purple pigment. The column is ochre with one dark red dorsal median nerve and two lateral fimbriate wings.

	Length (cm)	Width (cm)
Median sepal	0.45 - 0.7	0.2
Lateral sepal	0.4 - 0.45	0.3
Petal	0.25 - 0.6	0.1
Lip	0.4	0.15
Column	0.2	0.2

Flowering period September to April.

Distribution Crofts Mountain, Dolphin Head, Island View Hill, Catadupa, the Cockpit Country, Wilson Valley District, Aboukir, the John Crow Mountains and Plantain Garden River in Jamaica. Also found in Cuba and from Mexico to Costa Rica.

Cultural notes Keep well shaded under humid conditions. May be mounted on a tree-fern slab or potted in a medium of pea-sized charcoal.

Pleurothallis hirsutula

Description *Pleurothallis hirsutula* is epiphytic with slender, jointed, unifoliate stems arising from a basal rhizome which bears a cluster of fine roots. The stems are up to 5 cm tall, have three nodes with narrow sheaths, the two lowermost ones being covered with reddish-brown setae. The leaves are elliptic, dull green, leathery, flat on the upper surface; with the midrib prominent on the lower surface; they are up to 8 cm long and 1.5 cm wide. The petioles are tubular.

The inflorescence is a pendulous raceme bearing about six flowers and emerges through the top of the petiole most often lying on the upper surface of the leaf blade. The peduncle is zigzagged, up to 4.5 cm long and has a scarious sheath at the base. The flowers are dark reddish-purple, chinned and open partially.

The sepals are connate at the base to form a sepal cup, the lateral sepals being joined for almost their entire length. The sepals are ovate, apiculate, and have dark reddish-purple linear nerves banded closely together; translucent bands of tissue alternating with them at the base. The petals are diamond-shaped, clawed, have a jagged margin and are striped with linear reddish-purple nerves alternating with translucent bands; they embrace the column laterally.

The lip is fleshy, reddish-purple, ligulate with upright lateral lobes, rough-textured and arched against the column. The column is upright and extended into a foot about 0.2 cm long.

	Length (cm)	Width (cm)
Median sepal	0.8 - 1.0	0.2 - 0.4
Synsepalum	0.5 - 0.7	0.5
Petal	0.35	0.2
Lip	0.3	0.2
Column	0.4	–

Flowering period   May to August.

Distribution   Endemic. Hollymount, Mount Diablo and Balaclava.

Cultural notes   The plant may be mounted on a small hardwood twig or potted using pea-grain-sized charcoal or gravel as a medium. Keep well shaded.

Pleurothallis lanceola

Description   *Pleurothallis lanceola* is epiphytic and sometimes lithophytic with very short, unifoliate stems, about
0.5 cm tall, arising from a short rhizome. The plant is anchored
to the substratum by a thick bundle of roots. The leaves are
pale green, elliptic, notched at the apex, 2 - 2.5 cm long and
about 1 cm wide; the petioles are about 4 mm long. The
peduncle is filiform, 2.5 - 2.8 cm long and bears one flower at
the apex. The sepals and petals are orange. The median sepal
is concave and has three dark ochre nerves; the lateral sepals
are connate for most of their length, each has three linear,
reddish nerves and is spotted with red.

The petals are triangular, spathulate, narrow at the base
and each has two linear nerves. The lip is arched, reflexed,
blackish-red, thick and waxy and has one linear nerve. The
column is truncate and has a foot adnate to the lip. It has a pair
of pointed triangular wings, each with linear reddish nerves.

	Length (cm)	Width (cm)
Median sepal	0.6	0.3
Synsepalum	0.6	0.2
Petal	0.2	0.1
Lip	0.2	0.1
Column	0.2	–

Flowering period October to February.

Distribution Endemic. Found in Mount Moses, Mabess River, John Crow Peak and Balaclava.

Cultural notes The same as for *Pleurothallis corniculata*.

Pleurothallis nummularia

Description *Pleurothallis nummularia* is an epiphytic miniature with unifoliate stems about 2 mm long radiating from a short, branched rhizome and has fine slender roots anchoring it to the support plant. The leaves are spread out horizontally against the bark of the support plant stem; they are pale green, elliptic, thick-textured, up to 4 mm long and 3 mm wide.

A solitary filiform peduncle, about 3 mm long, covered by funnel-shaped sheathing bracts, is borne in the axil of each leaf. The flower buds are yellow and 2 mm long. The sepals are ovate, crystalline and yellow. The lip is reddish and pointed.

Flowering period March, July and August.

Distribution Rare. Found near Auchtembeddie in Jamaica. Also found in Cuba.

Cultural notes This plant will survive for a long period on the twig on which it was collected. No other cultural method may be recommended at this time. Keep well shaded and humid.

Pleurothallis oblongifolia

Description   *Pleurothallis oblongifolia* is epiphytic consisting of slender, unifoliate stems up to 6.5 cm tall, each having two nodes covered by tubular rigid sheaths. The leaves are olive-green, obovate, emarginate, leathery and tapered into a petiolate base; they are up to 8.5 cm long and 2.9 cm wide.

The inflorescence is a terminal raceme up to 16 cm tall and bears about eight flowers, each on a pedicel about 5 mm long. The flowers are dark reddish-purple and open only partially. The sepals have inrolled margins; the median sepal is ovate-lanceolate, the lateral sepals are lanceolate and connate with their apices free.

The petals are translucent with three linear dark red nerves; they are oblong and rounded at the apex. The lip has a background of pale green and is down-curving; it is trans-lucent, ligulate with two lateral lobes and has three dark red linear calli flanked by two shorter ones.

	Length (cm)	Width (cm)
Median sepal	1.0	0.25
Synsepalum	0.9	0.4
Petal	0.3	0.15
Lip	0.4	0.25
Column	0.3	–

Flowering period   August to January.

Distribution   St Andrew, Portland and St Thomas in Jamaica. Also found in Cuba and Hispaniola.

Cultural notes   The plant thrives when potted in a medium of tree fern and placed in a cool, shaded area.

Pleurothallis racemiflora

Description   *Pleurothallis racemiflora* is epiphytic or lithophytic with long, slender, jointed stems borne in tufts along
narrow, branching rhizomes. The stems are unifoliate, up to
14 cm long and longer covered by tubular sheathing scale
leaves. The leaves are ligulate, leathery, bright shiny green on
adaxial (upper) surfaces and dull green on abaxial surfaces, up
to 12 cm long and longer and 3 cm wide on average.

The inflorescence is a raceme arising from the axil of the leaf,
up to 30 cm long, but sometimes reaching 50 cm, bearing many
flowers at short intervals, all inclining in the same direction.
The flowers open partially, are translucent, pale greenish-yellow and aromatic of citrus. The lateral sepals are connate. The
petals are elliptic and the lip is ligulate. The column is minute
and narrow, projecting above the base of the lip.

	Length (cm)	Width (cm)
Median sepal	1.0	0.4
Lateral sepal	1.0	0.5
Petal	0.8	0.25
Lip	0.5	0.25
Column	0.3	–

Flowering period   September to March.

Distribution   Arntully, Bellevue, the Cockpit Country, Hardwar Gap, the Red Light District and St Ann in Jamaica. Also found in Puerto Rico and from Mexico to Panama.

Cultural notes   The plant is displayed to best advantage when mounted on tree-fern slabs because of the projection of the spikes which arch upwards. Basket culture using fine charcoal and leaf mould or bagasse is also recommended. Keep well shaded.

Pleurothallis ruscifolia

Description   *Pleurothallis ruscifolia* is epiphytic, lithophytic or grows in leaf mould. It has a cluster of slender, unifoliate, jointed stems up to 28 cm tall arising from a basal rhizome. The internodes are covered by tubular, papery brown sheathing scale leaves which have linear nerves. The leaves are elliptic-lanceolate, dark green, leathery, up to 11 cm long and 3.5 cm wide, and have a narrow petiole about 1.5 - 2 cm long.

The inflorescence is a fascicle in the axil of the leaf, subtended by a papery pouch-like bract; the pedicels are filiform, 0.7 - 1 cm long. The flowers are minute and number five to seven per fascicle; they are translucent, pale yellowish-green and open partially.

The lateral sepals are joined together to form a synsepalum which is identical in shape to the median sepal; they are deltoid, concave at the base and have tapered apices. The petals are very narrow and tapering but are shorter than the sepals. The lip has two lateral lobes, a triangular anterior lobe and a basal and an anterior ridge on the adaxial surface.

	Length (cm)	Width (cm)
Median sepal	0.2 - 0.5	0.2
Synsepalum	0.5	0.3
Petal	0.3	–
Lip	0.2	–
Column	0.1	–

Flowering period   June to August.

Distribution   St Ann and Hardwar Gap in Jamaica. Wider distribution in other Caribbean islands, Guatemala, Costa Rica, Panama and northern South America.

Cultural notes   Plants should be potted in a medium of charcoal and tree fern, and grown in shade in high humidity.

Pleurothallis sertularioides

Description *Pleurothallis sertularioides* is epiphytic forming a dense matting of stiff elliptic leaves arising at intervals on abbreviated stems borne along a thin, green, horizontal rhizome producing fine white roots. The leaves are 1.3 - 2.2 cm long and 5 mm wide. The stems are about 5 mm long, the flowers arising singly from the axils of the leaves on pedicels 5 - 8 mm. The flowers are translucent, pale green tinged with yellow and chinned at the base.

The median sepal is ovate-lanceolate, convex, and shields the column; the lateral sepals are arcuate and spreading. The petals are shorter than the sepals and grouped around the column; they have broad bases and tapering apices tinged with yellow.

	Length (cm)	Width (cm)
Median sepal	0.5	0.2
Lateral sepal	0.5	0.1
Petal	0.3	0.1
Lip	0.25	–
Column	0.15	–

Flowering period   July to November.

Distribution   The Cockpit Country and Hollymount. Also found in Mexico, Guatemala, Honduras, Cuba and Trinidad.

Cultural notes This plant makes a beautiful carpet of leaves and flowers when grown to specimen size. This is easy to accomplish because of its branching habit. The plant should be tied to a tree-fern slab or placed in a shallow basket with charcoal and tree fern. Keep in medium shade.

Pleurothallis tribuloides

Description *Pleurothallis tribuloides* is an epiphytic plant with short unifoliate stems, about 3 mm tall, growing in tight clusters and sheathed at the bases by cream-coloured scale leaves. The leaves are ligulate, leathery, emarginate, bright green, about 5.3 cm long and 1 cm wide. They are borne in groups of two or three arising from the axil of the leaf and sheathed by overlapping cream-coloured bracts, each bearing a single flower. The flower is bright orange or brick red and opens partially.

The sepals are finely setose on the outer surface and papillose on the inner surface near the apices. The lateral sepals are connate, forming a synsepalum which adheres to the median sepal at the tip, forming an aperture or window on either side. The median sepal is linear-lanceolate and the synsepalum ovate-lanceolate. The petals are ligulate and hooded at the apex. The lip is ligulate; the ovary finely setose.

	Length (cm)	Width (cm)
Median sepal	0.5	0.2
Synsepalem	0.6	0.2
Petal	0.2	0.1
Lip	0.2	–
Column	0.2	–

Flowering period   July to November.

Distribution   Found in many locations around Jamaica. A wider distribution extends from Mexico through Guatemala and Honduras to Cuba and Trinidad.

Cultural notes   The plant does well when grown in small pots in a medium of shredded tree fern and charcoal or in gravel. Keep well shaded.

Pleurothallis uncinata

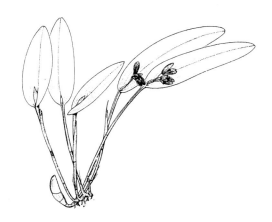

Description *Pleurothallis uncinata* is an epiphytic plant with jointed unifoliate stems about 20.5 cm long arising at intervals along a thick, creeping rhizome. The leaves are lanceolate, ribbed, dark green on the adaxial surfaces and light green underneath, up to 4.7 cm wide and 23.6 cm long; folded at the base and extended into a rigid tubular petiole.

One or two flowers are borne on a peduncle arising from the apex of the stem; the peduncle is about 3 cm long emerging at the top of the petiole. The sepals are fleshy, hairy, yellowish-green on abaxial surfaces, have several dark reddish nerves on the adaxial surfaces, are tinged with red at the base and spotted with red anteriorly. The petals are elliptic, yellowish-green and clawed at the base.

The lip is red and has a rounded anterior lobe and two triangular lateral lobes. The column is erect and yellow with a spot of red at the base.

	Length (cm)	Width (cm)
Median sepal	1.7	0.5
Lateral sepal	1.5	0.5
Petal	0.8	0.2
Lip	0.7	0.5
Column	0.6	0.2

Flowering period May to July.

Distribution Caledonia Peak, Port Royal Mountains, Fairy Glade, Hardwar Gap, Foxes' Gap and Portland in Jamaica. Also found in Venezuela, Costa Rica and Panama.

Cultural notes The same methods as for other *Pleurothallis* species.

Pleurothallis wilsonii

Description *Pleurothallis wilsonii* is an epiphytic plant having a slender creeping rhizome bearing sparse fine roots and unifoliate stems 1 - 1.5 cm tall at regular intervals along its length. The stems are covered with a papery tubular sheath at their bases. The leaves are stiff, leathery, elliptical and notched at the apices, olive on the adaxial surface and tinged with purple on the abaxial surface; they have a dark purple midrib.

The inflorescence is a pendent raceme bearing one to three partially-opened flowers and is protected by a folded papery bract at its base. The peduncle is 0.6 - 1.2 cm long. The sepals are translucent, ochre and are bordered on the margins by a dark purple nerve. The median sepal is ligulate and has three parallel dark purple nerves; the lateral sepals are connate, forming a synsepalum with a pouch at the base, the apex being rounded. The synsepalum has seven linear dark purple nerves. The petals are clawed, sagittate with a toothed margin, colourless, translucent and have a faint median magenta nerve.

The lip is scoop-shaped, ochre with two upright orange lateral lobes, the anterior lobe being fimbriate. The column lies parallel to the median sepal and is flanked by the petals. It is pale green with a dark reddish-purple base, the apex being bilobed with a toothed margin; it bears two pollinia.

	Length (cm)	Width (cm)
Median sepal	0.5	0.15
Synsepalem	0.4 - 0.5	0.3
Petal	0.25	0.1
Lip	0.3	0.2
Column	0.2	0.1

Flowering period August to November.

Distribution Crofts Mountain, Clarendon and Marshall's Pen in Jamaica. Also found in Puerto Rico and Guadeloupe.

Cultural notes This plant thrives well when tied to a stick or twig and suspended in a cool shaded area.

POLYSTACHYA

From the Greek *polys*, many and *stachys*, spike; a reference to the many branches or spikes on a single inflorescence in some species.

Polystachya concreta (extinctoria)

Description *Polystachya concreta* is epiphytic with short upright pseudobulbs each 1 - 1.3 cm tall, springing from an underlying rhizome and bearing two to four ligulate-lanceolate light green leaves which overlap at their bases in a rolled sheaf. The junction between leaf and pseudobulb is hidden by two or three papery sheathing scale leaves. The leaves are up to 23 cm long and 3.0 - 3.5 cm at their widest.

The inflorescence arises from the terminal axils of the leaves and consists of a number of spikelets each bearing about twenty-five flowers, all curving upwards from the rachis which has an average length of 35 cm and is covered in its entirety by papery sheathing bracts. The flowers are short-lived, non-re-supinate and open gradually towards the tip of the inflorescence; they are small with the lateral sepal and the lip forming an inverted chin.

The lateral sepals are triangular, pale green, waxy and fused laterally along the median axis of the flower; slightly concave at the margins with the apices divaricate. The lower median sepal is broadly ovate and projects towards the lip enclosing the minute column. The cream-coloured lip has a narrow basal isthmus 3 mm long which projects upwards adhering closely to the lateral sepals from which it bends sharply downwards where it expands into a four-lobed segment which curves out-wards. The petals are minute, elliptic and flank the column.

	Length (cm)	Width (cm)
Median sepal	0.3	0.25
Lateral sepal	0.4	0.4
Petal	0.3	0.025
Lip	0.4	0.4
Column	0.1 - 0.2	0.1

Flowering period   August to November.

Distribution   St Ann, St Andrew and St Catherine in Jamaica. Also found in Florida, Mexico to Brazil, Peru, the Bahamas and other Caribbean islands.

Cultural notes   The plant prospers on tree-fern slabs or in pots or baskets in charcoal or gravel. Keep in light shade.

PONTHIEVA

A reference to Henri de Ponthieu, an
eighteenth-century French West Indian merchant, who sent plant collections to Sir Joseph Banks in
England.

Ponthieva harrisii

Description   *Ponthieva harisii* is a terrestrial plant with a
cluster of basal leaves, the plant in flower measuring up
to 64 cm tall. The leaf blades are bright green, elliptical, have
a prominent midrib and slightly wavy margins, and are folded
at the base; they are up to 12 cm long and 4.5 cm wide. The
petioles are erect and up to 10 cm long. The scape is jointed and
has apiculate sheathing bracts at the nodes.

The inflorescence is a spike bearing numerous flowers (up to
eighty) arranged in an irregular spiral, the ovaries of the
earlier opening lower flowers developing into fruits (capsules)
before the topmost flowers have bloomed. The sepals and petals
are brownish-pink, translucent-crystalline, the sepals being
hairy on the abaxial surfaces; they point forwards in the flower
and encircle the lip. The median sepal is ligulate and concave,
the lateral sepals are arcuate and rounded at the apices. The

petals are ligulate and closely appressed to the sides of the median sepal.

The lip is trough-shaped, cream-coloured with green nerves on the lower half. It has three rounded anterior lobes. The column is green and adnate to the median sepal. The flowers are fragrant.

	Length (cm)	Width (cm)
Median sepal	0.5	0.1
Lateral sepal	0.6	0.1
Petal	0.5	0.1
Lip	0.6	0.3
Column	0.3	—

Flowering period   April to June.

Distribution   Arntully, St Catherine's Peak, the Red Light District, Bamboo and Hollymount in Jamaica. Also found in Hispaniola.

Cultural notes   This plant should be potted in a terrestrial mix and kept well shaded.

Ponthieva racemosa

Description   *Ponthieva racemosa* is terrestrial and grows in leaf mould. The leaves form a basal rosette and the roots are thick and cream-coloured. The former are light green, soft-textured and elliptic-lanceolate, the blades tapering at the bases into petioles which enfold the stem; they are up to 21 cm long and 4.8 cm wide. The scape is up to 60 cm long with bract-bearing nodes, the upper portion bearing short glandular hairs.

The inflorescence is a raceme with few to numerous flowers borne on pedicels 1.8 - 2.2 cm long ascending at about a 45° angle. The flowers are non-resupinate, the petals paired behind the median sepal forming a curved shield below the column. The sepals are pale green, the adaxial surfaces having white stripes. The median sepal is elliptic; the lateral sepals are ovate-apiculate and spread out horizontally with the top recurved. The petals are triangular, paired white with fine green stripes, clawed at the bases, the apices adhering to the apex of the median sepal.

The lip is green, trough-shaped with erect rounded lateral lobes and a white apiculate median lobe which points upwards.

The column is pale green, about 2.5 mm high with a brown triangular operculum opposite the petals and enclosing four cream-coloured pollinia. The stigma is at the apex of the column.

	Length (cm)	Width (cm)
Median sepal	0.6 - 0.7	0.3 - 0.35
Lateral sepal	0.7 - 0.8	0.4
Petal	0.6 - 0.8	0.45 - 0.5
Lip	0.6 - 0.7	0.6 - 0.9
Column	0.3	–

Flowering period November to March.

Distribution The Red Light District, Hollymount, the Tobolski Mines and the parishes of Manchester, Trelawny and Hanover in Jamaica. Also found in the other Greater Antillean islands.

Cultural notes Plant in leaf mould in pots providing good drainage and place in a shaded area.

Ponthieva ventricosa

Description   *Ponthieva ventricosa* is a terrestrial plant with a rosette of radical leaves. The leaves are lanceolate, apiculate, pale green, shiny, have reticulate venation and are up to 9.5 cm long and 3 cm wide. The scape is jointed, green, pubescent, with tubular bracts and is up to 48 cm long, bearing only a few flowers. The ovaries are pedicellate, pubescent, wider at the top and tapering towards the bases. The flowers are borne in a loose raceme at the top of the scape.

The sepals are white and pubescent on the abaxial surfaces; the median sepal is lanceolate and concave. The lateral sepals are triangular and each has a heavy band of green along the median vein on the abaxial surface and form a short chin around the spur of the lip. The petals are translucent, white and unequally bilobed. The lip forms a deep pouch near the base with the lateral lobes embracing the column and is patterned with green dots. The column is winged and has a stalked anther.

	Length (cm)	Width (cm)
Median sepal	0.35 - 0.5	0.15 - 0.2
Lateral sepal	0.4 - 0.5	0.2 - 0.3
Petal	0.35 - 0.5	0.1 - 0.2
Lip	0.35 - 0.6	0.2 - 0.4
Column	0.2 - 0.3	–

Flowering period   November to March.

Distribution   Clay and rock banks in the central parts of Jamaica and the Greater Antilles.

Cultural notes   A good terrestrial mix is adequate. Keep lightly shaded.

PRESCOTTIA

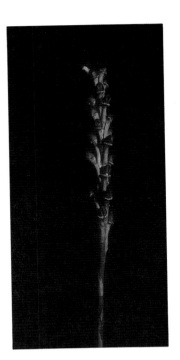

Named to houour John D. Prescott, an eighteenth/nineteenth century English botanist who travelled widely in northern Asia.

Prescottia oligantha

Description *Prescotia oligantha* is terrestrial with a basal rosette of about three leaves. It has hairy, tuberous, white roots sprouting from the base of the rosette. The leaves are ovate or elliptic-ovate, bright green, soft, shiny and have petioles between 0.5 and 3 cm long; the leaf blades being 4.5 - 9 cm long and 2.5 - 3.5 cm wide. The scape is up to 38 cm long, pinkish, glabrous and has green sheathing bracts at the nodes. The top of the scape is densely covered with up to seventy small sessile flowers, the ovaries being more conspicuous than the perianths and measuring about 4 mm in length. The flowers are non-resupinate, white, crystalline and translucent.

The sepals are ovate and all three are joined together at the base for about half their length to form a saccate pouch. The apices of the sepals are suffused with pink and strongly recurved; the lateral sepals are divergent, their apices flanking the lip on either side. The petals are linear, white and recurved at their apices. The lip is cucullate with the lateral lobes enfolding the green truncate column.

	Length (cm)	Width (cm)
Median sepal	0.2	0.15
Lateral sepal	0.2	0.1
Petal	0.15	0.1
Lip	0.2	0.2
Column	0.1	–

Flowering period January to April.

Distribution Between Cinchona and Morse's Gap, Knox College, Retford Pen, White Rock Hill, the Cockpit Country, Douglas Castle District, Uncommon Hill, the Blue Mountains, Green River Valley and Tweedside in Jamaica. Also found in Cuba, Puerto Rico, St Thomas, Guadeloupe and Dominica.

Cultural notes Plant in a mix as for other terrestrial orchids and keep well shaded.

Prescottia stachyodes

Description *Prescottia stachyodes* is a terrestrial plant with swollen, densely hairy roots and a basal rosette of leaves. The leaves have long reddish petioles up to 20 cm long; the leaf blades are ovate, apiculate, heart-shaped, puckered and up to 11 cm long and 7.7 cm wide.

The inflorescence is a spike with about fifty small flowers clustered at the tip of the peduncle. The peduncle is up to 75 cm tall, olive, tinged with brown and covered at the internodes by lanceolate, tubular sheaths. The flowers are each subtended by a bract which enfolds the pedicellate ovary. The sepals are green, lanceolate and are fused at the base to form a tan-coloured tube. The petals are linear and recurved at the tips.

The lip is uppermost in the flower and is thick, concave, incurved at the margins and overlaps the column leaving a small aperture at the front. The column is short and has two exposed pollinia.

	Length (cm)	Width (cm)
Median sepal	0.35	0.2
Lateral sepal	0.45	0.2
Petal	0.35	0.1
Lip	0.7	0.6
Column	0.2	–

Flowering period   September to May.

Distribution   The Tobolski mines, Hollymount, the Cockpit Country, Lydford, Arntully, John Crow Mountains and the Blue Mountain range in Jamaica. Also found from Guatemala to Brazil, Colombia, Ecuador, Peru and in other Caribbean islands.

Cultural notes   The plants may be potted in a medium of leaf mould and tree-fern fibre. Keep in medium shade.

SCHOMBURGKIA

Schomburgkia is dedicated to the nineteenth century German botanist Richard Schomburgk, who explored British Guiana (Guyana) with his brother Robert, and discovered the type material for this genus.

Schomburgkia lyonsii

Description Schomburgkias are largely epiphytic plants securely anchored by thick strong roots to rocks or branches of trees. Schomburgkia lyonsii has many fusiform, hardened pseudobulbs with distinct longitudinal grooves and at least six nodes. The pseudobulbs are borne at short intervals on a tough rhizome, are up to 60 cm tall with an average height of about 40 cm, each bearing one to three leathery, linear leaves with rounded apices which can be as long as 30 cm and are usually 5 cm wide.

The inflorescence is a raceme with the flowers inverted and borne in groups of ten to twenty-five on pale lavender pedicels 5 - 7 cm long, each subtended by a brownish-lavender bract 6.5 cm long. The peduncle arises from the axil of the leaves and is covered by stiff papery bracts for its entire length which may be between 100 - 143 cm. The sepals overlap the petals basally and both sets are oblong-ovate, have a greyish-white background which is heavily patterned with purple dots leaving a clear border around the undulate margins. The column is lilac, 1.1 cm long and curves downwards, the foot expanding basally into two lateral lobes forming a groove on the under surface.

The lip is roughly triangular with undulate margins, the side lobes raised and inrolled to fit into the curvature of the column. The underside of the outer lobe of the lip is heavily streaked with purple and the lateral margins are edged with yellow; the upper surface has three pairs of fine linear crests separated by a longer central one. The disc is spotted purple.

There is a close resemblance between the young plants of *Schomburgkia lyonsii* and *Encyclia fragrans* but the pseudobulbs of the former have a shinier appearance than those of the latter.

NB The inflorescence takes several weeks to develop but the flowers last only a day or two. This may indicate that they are self-pollinated as all the flowers form capsules which take a long time to mature. An alba form is known.

	Length (cm)	Width (cm)
Median sepal	2.5	1.1
Lateral sepal	2.1	1.1
Petal	2.5	1.1
Lip	1.7	1.4
Column	1.1	0.8

Flowering period August to November.

Distribution Rather widespread; Worthy Park, Hollymount, Arntully, the Cockpit Country, Trout Hall, Luidas Vale and Reynolds Mines in Jamaica. Also found in Cuba.

Cultural notes The plant thrives on tree-fern slabs but also thrives when mounted on the trunk of a tree or log in warm climates. Keep well illuminated.

Hybridization This plant has been hybridized with cattleyas, *Broughtonia*, laelias and epidendrums.

SPIRANTHES

From the Greek *speira*, coil and *anthos*, flower; referring to the twisted inflorescence of many species.

Spiranthes (Chondrorhynca) elata

Description   *Spiranthes elata* is a terrestrial plant with a rosette of basal leaves each up to 15 cm long and 4.5 cm wide. Fleshy, hairy roots sprout from the base of the rosette. The leaves are broadly ovate to elliptical and are always present at the time of flowering.

The scape is up to 40 cm tall with the flowers arranged in a terminal raceme. The flowers are greenish-white, sometimes tinged with brownish-pink, subtended by green bracts. The sepals are green and pubescent, the median sepal concave with a slight pouch at the base. The petals are lanceolate and paired.

The lip is green, glabrous, trough-shaped with a pair of rounded lateral lobes and a spathulate limb which is shallowly emarginate. It expands into a pouch at the base of the column which is upright.

	Length (cm)	Width (cm)
Median sepal	0.8	0.2
Lateral sepal	0.8	0.2
Petal	0.5	0.1
Lip	0.5 - 0.65	0.3
Column	0.4	–

Flowering period   February to April.

Distribution   Found near Luidas Vale, Stewart Town, Norwood District and Mount Diablo in Jamaica. A wider distribution is from Florida to Argentina, the Bahamas and other Caribbean islands.

Cultural notes   Use a terrestrial mix and keep in a cool, shaded area.

Spiranthes (Chondrorhynca) lanceolata

Description   *Spiranthes lanceolata* is a terrestrial plant 20 - 70 cm tall when in flower having a basal rosette of leaves and small tubers with hairy roots. The leaves are lanceolate and up to 30 cm long and 3.5 cm wide. The scape is up to 50 cm long, olive, hairy with pale green bracts and bears flowers in an apical raceme. The sepals are lanceolate, bright salmon-pink and hairy on the dorsal surfaces. The median sepal is much shorter than the lateral sepals and is concave at the base. The lateral sepals are arcuate with their tips curving upwards and are joined at the base to form a chin which encloses the base of the lip. The petals are arcuate, translucent, pink and closely appressed to the median sepal for their entire length.

The lip is pale pink, trough-shaped and densely hairy on its lower half, the rounded lateral lobes adhering to the sides of the column. The anterior lobe is acuminate and curves downward. The column is pink and is extended into a foot which is adnate to the ovary. There are two linear pollinia which point forward from the top of the column.

	Length (cm)	Width (cm)
Median sepal	2.5	0.9
Lateral sepal	3.3	0.8
Petal	2.2	0.5
Lip	2.6	1.1
Column	1.2	0.3

Flowering period   March to May.

Distribution   The Red Light District, Hollymount, the Tobolski Mines, Douglas Castle District, Lydford, Hunt's Pen, Adam Brandon's Patent, Windsor District and Big Level District in Jamaica. Also found in Florida, Mexico to Paraguay, the Bahamas and other Caribbean islands.

Cultural notes   Plant grows well in pots with a mix of fine charcoal, leaf mould, sifted bagasse and tree-fern fines. Keep in medium shade.

Spiranthes
(Chondrorhynca) speciosa

Description   *Spiranthes speciosa* is a terrestrial plant grow-ing in leaf mould. The plant has leaves arranged in a rosette, the innermost one spirally inrolled; the roots are thick and covered with fine white hairs. The leaves are light green with a dull sheen on the adaxial surface, elliptic, up to 10 cm long and about 6 cm wide; they are tapered and keeled at their bases.

The inflorescence is a spike with several flowers (about twenty-five) spirally arranged on the upper portion of a brownish-green rachis; the latter is completely covered by overlapping bracts and is up to 40 cm in larger specimens.

Each flower is subtended by a pink bract about 4 cm long. The flowers are tubular with the apices of the floral segments recurved; the ovary is pedicellate. The sepals are coral-pink, linear-ovate with very pointed apices and are saccate at the base. The lateral sepals are basally connate and overlap the median sepal which is attached to the back of the column. The two coral-pink petals are linear-elliptic with acute apices both meeting along the centre of the median sepal.

The lip is white, has two rounded basal lobes where it is articulated with the column foot and expands into two smaller lateral lobes which overlap the apex of the column. The column has a fine beak-like process at its apex and bears two linear pollinia; it has a small pink patch covered with fine white hairs on the underside below the stigma.

	Length (cm)	Width (cm)
Median sepal	1.5	0.55
Lateral sepal	1.6	0.4
Petal	1.4	0.35
Lip	1.6	0.6
Column	1.3	–

Flowering period   October to March.

Distribution   Worthy Park, St Ann, Portland, St Thomas, Banana Ground and Hollymount in Jamaica. Also found in Cuba, Hispaniola, Puerto Rico, southern Guatemala to Colombia and Venezuela.

Cultural notes   Plant grows well in pots with a mix of fine charcoal, leaf mould, sifted bagasse and tree-fern fines. Keep in medium shade.

STELIS

From the Greek *stelis*, little pillar. In Greek the word signifies the mistletoe which grows on trees and simulates the habit of this genus.

Stelis ophioglossoides

Description   *Stelis ophioglossoides* is an epiphytic plant which has a tight cluster of unifoliate, slender stems varying from 4 cm to 10.5 cm high arising from a branched rhizome. The roots are thin and numerous. The stems have two nodes each and the internodes are sheathed by long, tubular, ridged scale-leaves about 3 - 4.6 cm long. The leaves are dull green, leathery and linear-ligulate, up to 12 cm long and 1 - 2 cm wide.

The inflorescence is a raceme, two or three of these being borne in the leaf axil, each subtended by a minute bract. The sepals are translucent greenish-cream, deltoid and inrolled along the outer margins. The petals are dark red, minute and translucent. The lip is dark red, triangular, has upright lateral lobes and is grooved in the centre. The column is also minute and crimson.

	Length (cm)	Width (cm)
Median sepal	0.25	0.25
Lateral sepal	0.25	0.25
Petal	0.07	0.09 - 0.1
Lip	0.08	0.1

Flowering period   Year-round.

Distribution   Hollymount, Swift River and in the foothills of the John Crow Mountains in Jamaica. Also found in Cuba, Hispaniola, Dominica and Trinidad.

Cultural notes   Plant on strips of cedar or redwood shingle. May also be grown in pots in a mixture of charcoal and tree fern. Keep in medium shade.

TETRAMICRA

From the Greek *tetra*, fourfold
and *mikros*, small; referring to
the four minute pollinia in
addition to four larger ones.

Tetramicra parviflora

Description   *Tetramicra parviflora* is an epiphytic plant consisting of a set of shoots arising from a spreading stolon. The
roots are stout and sparse; the shoots are clustered, each
arising from the base of a neighbouring one. They are mostly
bifoliate, occasionally bearing an extra leaf and are narrowed
at the point of attachment. The leaves are dark green with a
suffusion of reddish purple pigment, elliptic, apiculate, keeled,
leathery, stiff and up to 2.5 cm long and 1 cm wide. The
peduncle is terminal, elongate, thin, rigid and bears a few
flowers; it is up to 15 cm long.

The sepals are lanceolate, buff-coloured and are speckled with amethyst. The petals are linear-lanceolate and also buff-coloured. The lip is trilobed and has a narrow isthmus fused to the column; the margin is crenate. The lateral lobes are spathulate, concave and striped with amethyst nerves. The column is club-shaped with a flattened head lying against the midlobe of the lip.

	Length (cm)	Width (cm)
Median sepal	0.6	0.2
Lateral sepal	0.7	0.2
Petal	0.6	0.1
Lip	0.5	1.3
Column	0.5	0.2

Flowering period   February to May.

Distribution   Auchtembeddie and the Cockpit Country in Jamaica. Also found in Hispaniola.

Cultural notes   This is best grown in a small pot with limestone gravel in a hot dry atmosphere.

VANILLA

From the Spanish *vanilla*, little pod, or sheath; a reference to the long slender, pod-like fruit in some species from which the spice is derived.

Vanilla claviculata

Description *Vanilla claviculata* is an epiphytic plant with long, stout, dull green, trailing stems about 1.4 cm in diameter. The stems have a shallow longitude groove on opposite sides, are angular at the nodes, each node having a short, curled root sprouting from it. The leaves are deciduous on older parts of the stems, sessile, shiny green and waxy, apiculate, up to 3.3 cm long and 1 cm wide.

The inflorescence is a stout, specialized lateral branch about 24 cm long with fragrant flowers being carried in a cluster at the apex and a few scattered along the main axis. The pedicels are stout and about 5 cm long. The sepals are elliptic, boat-shaped, fleshy and pale green with inrolled margins. The petals are pale green, wider than the sepals, spathulate with a cleft on the upper margins; they are keeled with the midrib protruding dorsally.

The lip is triangular, adnate to the lower half of the column to form a tube, the lateral lobes enfolding the rest of the column and having a fluted crenulate margin. Dorsally the lip is heavily streaked with purple, the lower half being pale green to cream and lined on the inside with short, white, silky hairs; it is white at the front and has two purple blotches on either side of the crest.

The crest has a small basal patch of white silky hairs and several rows of coarse, branched trichomes anteriorly. The column is curved with the stigmatic surface covered by the anther cap; three small lobes embrace the latter.

	Length (cm)	Width (cm)
Median sepal	4.7	1.3
Lateral sepal	4.8	1.7
Petal	4.6	1.7
Lip	5.1	5.2
Column	3.1	0.5

Flowering period   June to December.

Distribution   Found in the Portland lighthouse area, alumina mud-lake dam area, Mount Rosser, Island View Hill (Trelawny), Worthy Park and Bull Savannah. Also found in the Greater Antilles and Grand Cayman.

Cultural notes   It is best to plant the cut end of the stem in earth and support the rest on a trellis, exposing the plant to very bright light.

Vanilla fragrans (planifolia)

Description   *Vanilla fragrans* is an epiphytic plant with stout stems about 1 cm in diameter and having internodes up to 13 cm long. One or two roots are borne at each node. The leaves are pendulous along the stem, are planar, thick, oblong- lanceolate, shiny green, up to 21 cm long and 5.5 cm wide. The flowers are borne in axillary racemes which elongate up to 10 cm as the flowers mature. The flowers are green, fleshy, fragrant, have pedicellate ovaries and open only partially.

The sepals are lanceolate, pale green, waxy and slightly keeled. The petals are pale green with a median ridge on the abaxial surface and are sometimes notched near the apices. The lip is adnate to the column for about half of its length where it forms a narrow basal tube. The front lobe of the lip is flared and lined with numerous yellow calli. There is a protuberance about 0.5 cm long, densely covered with trichomes found on the centre of the lip lying below the column. The column has a recurved apex about 0.5 cm long with the pollinia lying under its surface and protected laterally by two column wings. The stigma is protected by an operculum. The fruit is a capsule and is 15 - 25 cm long.

	Length (cm)	Width (cm)
Median sepal	5.7	1.0
Lateral sepal	5.5	1.2
Petal	5.6	1.0
Lip	5.2	2.6
Column	4.5	0.3

Flowering period   February to late in the year.

Distribution   Spring Garden, Cambridge and Mount Charles Estate in Jamaica. Also found in Mexico, Belize, Guatemala, Costa Rica and Florida.

Cultural notes   The same as for *V. claviculata*.

Vanilla wrightii

Description   *Vanilla wrightii* is an epiphytic plant with stout vining stems; the leaves are borne singly, each opposite to a single root at the nodes; the internodes being 5 - 11 cm long. The leaves are elliptic, leathery, dark green with distinct brown margins and petioles. The inflorescence is a terminal raceme with about three flowers, each flower being borne on a pedicel up to 5 cm long. The flowers open sequentially. The sepals and petals are tan-coloured, the petals are paler than the sepals, elliptic and translucent. The sepals are fleshy, the lateral sepals elliptic arcuate and thickened at the tips, the median sepal elliptic. The lip is triangular, narrow and fleshy at the base but with a papery texture in the wider flared area; it is golden-yellow with paired white blotches at the base and has several crests in the centre. The lateral lobes of the lip are adnate to the column for most of its length. The column is long, narrow and pale-orange.

	Length (cm)	Width (cm)
Median sepal	6.0	1.0
Lateral sepal	6.0	1.0
Petal	6.5	0.7
Lip	6.5	3.8
Column	4.0	0.6

Flowering period   March, July.

Distribution   Foxes' Gap in Jamaica. Also found in Guyana, Surinam, Cuba, Hispaniola and Trinidad.

Cultural notes   A difficult plant, but it seems to like wet, shady areas. A pot with a totem pole of tree-fern wrapped in sphagnum works reasonably well for supporting this vining plant.

XYLOBIUM

From the Greek *xylon*, wood or log and *bios*, life; referring to the epiphytic habit of plants in this genus.

Xylobium palmifolium

Description *Xylobium palmifolium* is epiphytic and also occasionally found in leaf mould or on rocks. It has dark green pseudobulbs, each supported on a short, thick, brown stem, emerging at close intervals from an underlying rhizome and covered at the base by large, desiccated, fibrous, brown, over-lapping scale leaves. The pseudobulbs are unifoliate, cylindrical at their bases and tapering at their apices.

The leaves are stiff, shiny, dark green, elliptic-lanceolate, sometimes pendent and up to 1.8 cm long and 9.5 - 10.5 cm wide; they are furrowed on the adaxial surfaces along five main veins.

The petioles are terete, grooved and up to 11.5 cm long and 6 mm wide. They are furrowed on the adaxial surfaces along five main veins and are sometimes pendent. The scape is cream-coloured, up to 11 cm long and covered along the lower half by imbricating brown bracts. The flowers are pale yellow and are borne on pedicels about 2.1 cm long, each subtended by a linear bract.

The lateral sepals are triangular, tapering to a pointed apex; they are basally connate where they are fused to the underside of the column and they overlap the underside of the lip. The median sepal is linear-lanceolate and attached behind the column apex. The petals are linear-lanceolate and are attached to the upper end of the column where they flank the median sepal.

The lip is spathulate and narrowed at the base where it is attached to the column foot. It is incurved where it is appressed to the column, the anterior lobe curving downward; the anterior margin is crenulate. The column is extended into a column foot which curves outwards and forms a mentum with the lip.

	Length (cm)	Width (cm)
Median sepal	1.9	0.4
Lateral sepal	1.9	0.2
Petal	1.6	0.35
Lip	1.6	0.8
Column	1.25	0.4

Flowering period   July to September.

Distribution   The Cockpit Country, Hardwar Gap, Silver Hill Gap, St Catherine's Peak and Hollymount in Jamaica. Also found in the Dominican Republic, Cuba and Trinidad.

Cultural notes   The plant flourishes in a basket containing a mixture of charcoal and leaf mould. Keep in medium to heavy shade.

GLOSSARY

abaxial	Referring to the surface or side of an organ away from the axis; dorsal.
acuminate	Having a gradually tapering point; the margins concave near the tip.
acute	Distinctly and sharply pointed; margins straight to convex.
adaxial	Towards the tip of the axis, inner or upper sides of leaves and bracts.
adnate	Fusion of unlike parts; cf. connate.
anther	That part of the stamen which produces pollen.
anther cap	A roof-like extension over the anther cells.
antrorse	Directed upwards or forwards; opposed to retrorse.
apical	At the tip; from the apex.
apiculate	Having or terminating in an apiculus.
apiculus (-li)	A sharp, short point.
appressed	Lying flat or closely pressed against a structure; adpressed.
approximate	Close together.
arcuate	Bent like a bow; curved.
articulate	Jointed; attached at a joint.
attenuate	Gradually tapering to a narrow point; cf. acuminate.
auricle	An ear-like lobe.
auriculate	Eared; having the form of an ear.
axil	The angle formed between an axis and any structure arising from it, as in the phrase, "in the axil of the leaf".
axis	The central or main stem of a plant or inflorescence.
bifid	Having one cleft and two lobes.
bifoliate	Bearing two leaves.
bifurcate	Forked at the top.
bilobate	With two lobes.
bilobed	*See* bilobate.
bract	A scale- or sheath-like structure homologous with a leaf, but lacking a distinct blade and usually found subtending a flower in an inflorescence.
bracteole	A small bract situated upon the stalk of a flower.
bulb	A body composed of circular, concentric leaf-bases, all attached to a disc-like or dome-like stem.
callus (-li)	A crest or fleshy outgrowth of the lip.
capitulum (-la)	A head of sessile flowers.
capsule	A several-parted, dehiscent (splitting) dry fruit.
carina (-e)	A keel.
caudicle	A slender, tail-like outgrowth of a pollinium.

ciliate	Fringed with hairs; bearing hairs along the margin.
claw	A narrow stalk-like part of a floral segment.
cleistogamous	Referring to a flower fertilizing itself without opening.
column	The central structure in an orchid flower comprising the union of style, stamen and stigma.
column foot	Ventral extension of the base of the column which has the lip attached at its tip.
concave	With the outline or surface curved like the interior of a circle or sphere.
conduplicate	Referring to leaves, petals, sepals, etc., with halves folded together lengthwise.
connate	A fusion of like parts. *See* adnate.
connivent	Coming into contact or converging, but not fused.
convex	Having a more or less rounded surface.
cordate	Indented at the base; more or less heart-shaped.
corm	An upright thickened underground stem in which food and water are stored.
crenate	Scalloped; shallowly round-toothed.
crenulate	With small scallops.
crest	A ridge, generally on a floral part, sometimes cut and fringed.
cucullate	Hooded; wide at the top, drawn to a point below; a conical roll of paper, for example.
cuneate	Wedge-shaped.
deciduous	Falling off; as leaves.
decurrent	Running into or extending downwards, usually involving the adnation of parts.
decurved	Curved downwards.
deflexed	Bent outwards or downwards; reflexed, opposite of inflexed.
dehiscent	The property of capsules to split open.
deltate	*See* deltoid.
deltoid	Shaped like an equilateral triangle or Greek letter delta.
disc	A more or less rounded flattened structure; in orchids referring particularly to the median or basal portion of the lip.
distal	Away from or towards the opposite end of the axis or base. *See* proximal.
distichous	Two-ranked; having leaves or other organs in two opposite rows in the same plane as opposed to spiral or whorled.
divaricate	Extremely divergent or widely spaced.
dorsal	Back; referring to the back or outer surface of a part or organ; abaxial, opposite of ventral.
ellipsoid	A solid of which every plane section is an ellipse or a circle; resembling an ellipse, spindle-shaped.
elliptic	Shaped like an ellipse; oval in outline, oblong with regularly rounded ends and widest at the middle; spindle-shaped.

emarginate	With a shallow notch at the apex; retuse.
endemic	Native in or confined to a restricted area.
epiphyte	Any plant which grows on another plant for support.
equitant	Said of conduplicate or laterally flattened leaves which overlap each other in two ranks.
exserted	Protruded beyond; sticking out.
falcate	Sickle-shaped.
fascicle	A cluster or bundle.
filament	In a "typical" stamen, the stalk bearing the anther.
filiform	Thread-like; long and slender.
fimbriate	Fringed; said of a margin rimmed by long, slender processes.
flavescent	Yellowish.
foot	*See* column foot.
fractiflex	Zigzagged.
fusiform	Spindle-shaped; slender.
glabrous	Not hairy; without pubescence.
glaucous	Covered with a bloom; with a whitish, bluish or bluish-green coating, often waxy and which can be rubbed off.
imbricate	Overlapping, as roofing shingles.
inflorescence	The flower (if solitary) or flower cluster of a plant. *See also* capitulum, fascicle, spike, raceme, umbel.
internode	That segment of a stem between two nodes.
keeled	Ridged, like the bottom of a boat or breast of fowl.
keiki	An offset or offshoot of a plant produced vegetatively; from the Hawaiian for "baby".
labellum	*See* lip.
lamina (-nae)	The expanded leaf-blade as opposed to the narrowed petiole (leaf stalk).
lanceolate	Lance-shaped; said of leaves with the greatest width about one-third from the base and tapering to the apex.
lateral sepal	The left- or right-hand sepal, the two of which may be wholly or partly fused to form a synsepalum, q.v., in some orchid flowers.
ligulate	Strap-shaped; also "ligular", "lingulate".
limb	The expanded flat portion of a sepal or petal in some flowers.
linear	Narrow and comparatively long, with parallel margins or sides.
lip	One of the three petals which is usually larger and differently shaped and often differently coloured from the other two; the median petal or labellum.
lithophyte	Any plant growing on rocks.
lobe	A segment of tissue that represents a division almost to the middle of an organ.
median sepal	The middle, upper or dorsal sepal.

mentum	A chin-like extension at the base of the flower made up of the column foot and the lateral sepals.
monopodial	A growth habit in which the same growing point continues the elongation of the shoot indefinitely, bearing axillary inflorescences. *See* sympodial.
mucronate	Possessing a sharp, abrupt, terminal point.
mycorrhiza	Fungi that are symbiotically associated with the new seedlings, synthesizing simple sugars for their use, and which eventually inhabit the roots.
nodding	Bent or drooping downwards.
node	That part or joint of a stem where one or more leaves is attached.
non-resupinate	Referring to orchid flowers in which the lip is uppermost.
oblong	At least twice as long as broad with nearly parallel sides.
obtuse	Blunt or rounded at the end.
operculum	Lid.
ovary	The basal extension of the column below the perianth (sepals and petals) which contains the ovules; the ovule-bearing part of a "typical" pistil.
ovate	Shaped like a longitudinal section of a hen's egg with the broader end basal.
ovule	The primordial seed.
pandurate	Fiddle-shaped, as of a leaf.
panicle	An inflorescence, the main axis of which is branched and whose branches bear loose flower clusters.
papilla (-lae)	A soft, superficial gland or protuberance.
pedicel	The stalk of an individual flower in an inflorescence.
pedicellate	Produced on a pedicel; that which has a pedicel.
peduncle	The stalk of an inflorescence.
peloric	The abnormal reversion of the lip to a form like that of the other petals.
peltate	Said of leaves or other plane structures which are attached to a stalk inside the margin, and are umbrella or shield-shaped.
pendent	Hanging down from a support.
pendulous	Hanging pendent (downward).
perianth	A collective term for the sepals and petals together.
petal	Commonly white or coloured (rarely green) floral part borne above or within the sepals; in orchids two of the three inner or upper perianth parts, the third being called the lip.
petiole	The narrow, stem-like basal part of a leaf; the leaf stalk.
pinnate	With leaflets, veins or other structures arranged oppositely along a central axis as in a feather.
pistil	The central organ of flowers in the basal portion, or ovary, of which the ovules containing the eggs are produced; usually considered as the "female" or seed-bearing component of the flower. *See* stamen.

plicate	Pleated or folded as a fan; usually referring to leaves with several to many longitudinal and raised veins (nerves).
pollen	The grains or mass formed in an anther and normally deposited on the stigma, through which they send a tube to the ovary carrying the male gametes.
pollinium(-ia)	A more or less compact and coherent mass of pollen usually the contents of an anther cell or one half of an anther cell.
proximal	Nearer to or towards the axis or base. *See* distal.
pseudobulb	A thickened stem, usually aerial, which stores food and water. *See* bulb.
pubescent	Provided with short hairs; downy.
raceme	An unbranched inflorescence in which pedicellate (stalked) flowers normally open from the base upwards.
recurved	Bent or curved backwards or downwards.
resupinate	Pedicel twisted 180°; flowers having the lip on the lower side. The typical position in orchids.
reticulate	Of veins or markings forming a network.
retrorse	Directed backwards or downwards towards the base; opposite of antrorse.
revolute	Rolled back from, that is, under the margins or apex towards the lower or abaxial side.
rhizome	Generally a horizontal stem on or in the substrate.
rosette	A densely clustered spiral of leaves borne near the ground
rostellum	A beak-like portion of the stigma which aids in gluing pollinia to the pollinating agent; the tissue barrier which separates the anther from the receptive stigma in the same flower.
saccate	Sac-like; deeply concave, bag-shaped, pouchy.
sagittate	Usually said of leaves which are enlarged at the base into two acute, straight, downwardly pointing lobes like the barbed head of an arrow.
saprophytic	Obtaining nourishment from non-living organic matter.
scape	A leafless floral axis or peduncle.
scarious	Thin, dry and membranous; not green.
sepal	Usually the outer green perianth segments of a flower; in orchids, the outer three perianth segments which are often coloured.
serrate	Said of leaves or other plane parts that are beset with antrorse (forward pointing) teeth along the margin; saw-toothed.
sessile	Without a stalk.
seta (-tae)	A bristle.
setose	Bristly; bearing or covered with bristles.
shoot	A stem bearing leaves and other appendages.
spathulate	Oblong with the basal end narrowed as in a spatula or spoon; spatula or spoon-shaped. Also "spatulate".

spike	An elongated, usually unbranched inflorescence in which sessile flowers open from the base upwards.
spur	A slender, tubular or sac-like projection from a flower part, usually producing nectar; commonly formed by the base of the lip.
stamen	The pollen-bearing portion of a seed plant. Sperms are produced by the germinating pollen grains conventionally considered as the "male" component of the flower.
stigma	The sticky, receptive part of the pistil which receives the pollinia (pollen masses).
style	In a "typical" pistil, the narrowed "neck" joining the basal ovary with the apical stigma.
subtend	To stand below or close to, as a bract beneath a flower.
symbiosis	An intimate, usually anatomical and mutually beneficial relationship between individuals of different species.
sympodial	A growth habit in which each successively produced shoot has limited growth; new shoots arise periodically from new growing points at the bases of old ones.
synsepalum	A compound organ formed by the fusion of the two lateral sepals in some orchids.
terete	Circular in transverse section; cylindric and usually tapering.
terrestrial	Said of a plant rooted in the soil and/or humus layer.
trichome	A hair, bristle, scale or other epidermal appendage.
trilobate	With three lobes.
trilobed	Three-lobed.
triquetrous	Three-edged; with three prominent angles, three-angled in cross-section.
umbel	An inflorescence in which a cluster of pedicels (flower stalks) arises from the same point like the ribs of an umbrella; flowers open sequentially from the outside inwards.
undulate	Wavy; up and down, not in and out.
unifoliate	Bearing a single leaf.
velamen	The absorbent epidermis of the roots of epiphytic orchids.
ventral	Front; referring to the inner surface of a part or organ: adaxial, opposite of dorsal, q.v.
verrucose	Having warty elevations.
viscidium (-dia)	A sticky, clearly defined part of the rostellum which is removed with the pollinia (pollen masses) as a unit and serves to attach the pollinia to an insect or other pollinating agent.
wing	Generally a thin appendage or ridge on a stem, capsule or other part.
xerophytic	Growing in and suited to a dry environment.
zygomorphic	Bilaterally symmetrical.

Bibliography

Adams, C. Dennis. 1970. "*Broughtonia.* A brief Review." *The Florida Orchidist* 13: 8-11.

Adams, C. Dennis. 1971. "*Broughtonia* again." *The Florida Orchidist* 14: 101-105.

Adams, C. Dennis. 1972. *Flowering Plants of Jamaica.* University of the West Indies. Mona. Jamaica.

Arditti, J. 1969. "Floral Anthocyanins in Some Orchids." *Amer. Orch. Soc. Bull.* 38: 407-413.

Bechtel, H., E. Launert, and P. Cribb. 1986. *The Manual of Cultivated Orchids.* Blandford Press. Poole.

Dunsterville, G. C. K., and L. A. Garay. 1959. *Orchids of Venezuela.* Vol 1. Andre Deutsch. London.

Fawcett, W., and A. B. Rendle. 1910. "Orchidaceae." In *Flora of Jamaica.* Vol. 1. British Museum. London.

Garay, L. A., and H. Sweet. 1974. "Orchidaceae." In *Flora of the Lesser Antilles Orchidaceae.* Harvard Univ. Press. Cambridge.

Hawkes, A. D. 1965. *Encyclopaedia of Cultivated Orchids.* Faber & Faber. London.

Hespenheide, H. A. 1968. "*Lepanthes:* A revision of the West Indian species of *Lepanthes.*" *Nat. Sci. Philad.* 120: 1-23; 33-39.

Luer, Carlyle. 1972. *The Native Orchids of Florida.* New York Botanical Garden. Bronx.

Moir, W. W. G. 1978. *Breeding the Oncidium. Sect. Oncidium* (erroneously the equitant-variegate *Oncidiums*). *Orchid Digest* 42: 85-91.

Northen, Rebecca T. 1988. *Miniature Orchids.* Van Nostrand Reinhold Co. Princeton.

Powell, Dulcie. 1972. "The Botanic Garden, Liguanea." *Bulletin of the Institute of Jamaica* (Science Series) 15, Pt 1: 1-94.

Sauleda, R. P., and R. M. Adams. 1989. "Revision of the West Indian Genera *Broughtonia, Cattleyopsis* and *Laeliopsis.*" *Orchid Digest* 53: 39.

Schultes, R. E. 1960. *Orchids of Trinidad & Tobago.* Pergamon Press. New York.

Schultes, R. E., and A. S. Pease. 1963. *Generic Names of Orchids.* Academic Press. New York.

Schweinfurth, Charles. 1983. *Flora de Cuba, Orchids* (Reprint). Havana.

Index

Species that are described appear in bold italic; the genus as well as those plants that are merely mentioned appear in normal italic.